THE HYPERACTIVE CHILD

THE
HYPeR
AcTIVE
CHiLD

DR. GRANT L. MARTIN

VICTOR BOOKS

A DIVISION OF SCRIPTURE PRESS PUBLICATIONS INC.
USA CANADA ENGLAND

Scripture quotations are from the Holy Bible, New International Version®. *Copyright © 1973, 1978, 1984 by International Bible Society. Used by permission of Zondervan Publishing House. All rights reserved.*

Copyediting: Carole Streeter and Barbara Williams

Cover Design: Joe DeLeon

Cover Illustration: Gary Locke

Library of Congress Cataloging-in-Publication Data

Martin, Grant.
  The hyperactive child / by Grant Martin.
    p.   cm.
  Includes bibliographical references.
  ISBN 0-89693-068-8
  1. Attention-deficit hyperactivity disorder — Popular works. 2. Attention-deficit hyperactivity disorder — Treatment. 3. Hyperactive children.
  I. Title.
  RJ506.H9M423   1992
  618.92'8589 — dc20   *92-18310*
                                                                          CIP

---

    3   4   5   6   7   8   9   10   Printing/Year   96   95   94   93

CONTENTS

INTRODUCTION

Some children can't sit still. They appear distracted by every little thing and don't seem to learn from their mistakes. These children disregard rules, even when they are punished repeatedly. They also tend to act without thinking, and this results in many accidents and reprimands.

Maybe you know a child like this. Perhaps you *have* a child who seems "hyper" or distractible. This book is about children who have problems with attention, impulse control, and overarousal. This collection of problematic features is called *attention-deficit hyperactivity disorder* (ADHD). Here are a few examples of experiences common with ADHD children:

> Whenever we take Fred out in public, we spend all of our time reminding him to sit down or be quiet. He never stops. He's impossible to take to church, so we've about decided not to go anymore. He's always moving ninety miles an hour.

> Sally daydreams constantly. We know she's bright, yet she's flunking several of her classes. The other day her dad and I struggled with her for several hours to get her homework done. At first she said she didn't have any. We checked her notebook and found the assignment sheet. She was tearful, but we finally completed the two pages of math. And would you believe it, the next day we got a call from her teacher telling us Sally hadn't turned in her work.

> I hate to pick Terry up at school. It seems that every day his teacher is telling me about Terry talking out in class, making animal noises, or getting out of his seat. He's only six years old, but I'm afraid he's already beginning to dislike school. I feel it's all my fault.

ADHD is one of the most common reasons children are referred to mental health professionals. It may be one of the most prevalent problems of childhood. The consensus of professional opinion is that approximately 3 to 5 percent of children have ADHD. This translates to as many as 2 million school-age children. Every classroom in the country averages one ADHD child.

What is the problem here? Why do these children impulsively go from one activity to another? Whatever the reasons, ADHD makes family life very disruptive and stressful. No matter how hard parents of ADHD children try to do the right thing, their children persist in daydreaming, missing homework assignments, and neglecting chores.

Raising any child is difficult. But the burden seems overwhelming when a child fails to respond to normal methods. This "difficult" child continues to struggle with school, can't make or keep friendships, and becomes increasingly discouraged. Notes from the teacher and complaints from other parents about the inattentive and overactive child add to the parents' consternation.

Perhaps you are one of these disheartened parents. You've tried everything, but can't seem to get your child to settle down. This book is written for your aid and comfort. We know a great deal about attention disorders. Because of extensive research, much has been identified about the prevalence, developmental nature, prognosis, and treatment of ADHD. At this point there is no known cure. However, enough is understood about management to make the life of an ADHD child much less frustrating. And with that help, you as a parent can be more free of guilt and anxiety.

I have spent over twenty-five years working with children and their families. In that time, I have served as a school psychologist, classroom teacher, special education researcher, and clinician. I estimate that I have dealt with almost 6,000 children. Over the last seventeen years in private practice as a child psychologist, I have completed hundreds of evaluations concerning the emotional and educational status of children. Many of these children had the features of attention deficit and hyperactivity.

It is from this base of experience that I have written this book. I will be combining the best ideas of known authorities in the field with my own experience to give you a practical resource. There are three parts to this book. In Part One, we will look at the process of identifying an ADHD child. Some children have attentional and motivational problems along with overactive behavior patterns. Other attention-disordered children do not have any overt features of hyperactivity. We will present the current best definitions of ADHD and tools for screening your child. If it looks as if your child may have some of the characteristics of ADHD, you will find helpful the section on multidisciplinary evaluation, as well as the current opinions about the causes and sources of attention disorders. A summary of genetic and environmental factors will help you understand how your child may have come to have this problem. Some of the myths of ADHD will also be identified and explained.

Part Two will focus on treatment and intervention. Stimulant medication is often recommended for ADHD children. There are many legitimate questions about the use of medication in treating ADHD. We will examine the pros and cons of using medication, and the place of diet and other physical strategies. ADHD demands a whole-person approach; medication alone is seldom sufficient. "Skills, not pills" is an important slogan here. Therefore, I will highlight several forms of intervention. Parental styles or deficiencies do not cause ADHD. But some types of parental reactions can exaggerate or intensify the problems of an ADHD child. Many specific suggestions will be given to help you regain control.

Part Two will also present ideas for teaching self-control and social skills to the child who struggles with impulsivity and failure to follow rules. The difference between incompetency and noncompliance is important. We will discuss this difference and how it applies to the ADHD child.

Educational issues in treatment are very critical, since 40 to 60 percent of all ADHD children also have learning difficulties of some type. The implications for class placement and instruction will be discussed. Children with ADHD have chronic problems with incomplete homework, and disorganization. I will suggest ways to help reduce these hassles and help bring about more success at school.

The last topic in Part Two is spiritual issues—the place and forms of prayer, maintaining patience, and keeping your own spiritual balance.

Part Three contains resources for the home and school. Educational materials for both the child and parent are listed, as well as names and addresses of various support groups and sources of additional information about ADHD.

The labels for ADHD are confusing. I used *hyperactive* in the title because it is common in our daily jargon. Technically, hyperactivity is only one feature of attention deficit hyperactive disorders. Many children have difficulty with inattention and distractibility, but are not hyperactive. I may use the term *hyperactivity* in the generic sense. Most of the time, I will use ADHD or *attention deficit* as the general term.

Many more boys than girls appear to have ADHD. For this reason I have chosen to use the male designation in most of my descriptions. It may be that girls are underidentified at this point, partly because they tend to be daydreamers rather than "hyper" or aggressive.

Attention deficit hyperactivity disorder is a very real problem that affects millions of children. Certainly not all disruptive or active children have ADHD. It is important to know the differences. My prayer is that this book will help you become a more informed and confident parent or teacher. God desires a life of abundance for every child. The goal of this book is to help your child grow toward that potential.

This book was written not only to expand your knowledge about ADHD, but also to give you resources where you can obtain more information when you need it. In light of this purpose, I need to say something about the Reference pages at the ends of chapters.

As you read, you will see that the footnote numbers are not always in sequential order; also, you may see the same number two or three times in a chapter. Some of the items function as footnotes, indicating page numbers. But others are there to give you the sources of information. I hope they will be helpful to you.

Grant L. Martin, Ph.D.
Seattle, Washington
1992

PART ONE

IDENTIFICATION OF ADHD

"I do not understand what I do. For what I want to do I do not do, but what I hate I do."

Romans 7:15

ChAPTER ONE

DO I HAVE A HYPERACTIVE CHILD?
Definition and Characteristics of ADHD

The tiger perched silently on the ledge overhanging the earthen trail below. His tail waved fitfully in the thick jungle air. A gray mist partially concealed the images of the adventurers inching their way toward the hungry cat. The bullet hole in his thigh served to intensify his rage and lust for a kill. The humans in expedition gear had no forewarning of the fate that awaited them. Then, just as the intruders passed under the ledge . . .

"Andrew, have you picked up your coat yet?" his mother called from the kitchen. "I told you thirty minutes ago to take your coat to your room. What on earth have you been doing all this time? Turn off that TV and do what I told you this very minute."

"But Mom," Andrew wailed from the family room where he was engrossed in the video game his uncle had given him for his birthday. "I'm in the middle of my Forbidden City adventure game. I'm at the third level and I've got 5,000 points. If I quit now, I'll lose!"

"I don't care where you are or how many points you have. Turn off that game and do what I told you or else I'll take it away and you won't play with it until you're twenty-one years old," Andrew's mother threatened.

Then turning back to her casserole preparation, Andrew's mother muttered to herself, "I will never understand how he can sit in front of that stupid TV for hours and play silly video games without batting an eye. And yet when I ask him to do something, he can't concentrate for more than two minutes. What is the matter with him?"

Does this sound familiar? For many parents of children with attention disorders, this vignette is a common occurrence. There are over 12 million people in the United States who have difficulties with attention, impulsivity, and over-arousal. The current term for this collection of features is *attention-deficit hyperactivity disorder* (ADHD). No one seems to know why these individuals can't pay attention. They are accused of being lazy, disobedient, willful, immature, or even demon-possessed. Left untreated, this developmental disorder disrupts a child's life and results in low self-esteem, poor grades, and social and emotional problems. Many of these features will not be outgrown without help. Imagine the impact of this description following a child throughout his school years.

> He won't finish his work. He bothers other children. He's overactive and won't keep his hands to himself. He won't follow rules or do what you tell him. One minute he's happy and the next minute he is angry. The slightest event will provoke an outburst. He does not stop and think before he blurts out answers. Other children don't like to have him around. He's excitable and disruptive in class. He has practically no friends. His behavior is intolerable. Something has to be done to make this child behave.[9]

If your child is having some of these problems at home, in school, and with his peers, you are concerned. It's also likely you are frustrated, and even frightened, because you don't know how to make things better for your son or daughter. Friends and family have offered all types of suggestions. You may have tried some of these ideas with limited or no success, and then have blamed yourself for your child's problems. Some family members say you need to be more firm and consistent. Others imply you are spoiling your child. You're told all he needs is a good spanking.

These well-meaning folks don't understand how difficult things are with your child. They don't realize that exclusively punitive methods just make him more aggressive.

It is difficult not to take on some feelings of blame and guilt. You believe you should be able to manage your child more effectively. There must be something wrong with you or your parenting skills to produce such a problem child. It's very natural that you would feel this way. Many parents of children with attention deficits have experienced the same range of emotions.

You also may have felt anger and resentment toward your child. You want him to respect and obey you, and you tend to take some of his misbehavior personally. Why does he always seem to be testing you? Sometimes you think he could embarrass the stripes off a zebra with the errors and accidents you have experienced. It seems this child of yours has a life mission to make you miserable. You bet you have taken these actions personally!

This anger also can become intense and frightening. Your patience is exhausted, the chores still aren't done, and you are nose-to-nose arguing about the status of the hamster cage. In the middle of this, your child calls you a demeaning name and your emotions cut loose. You slap him across the face, and he runs screaming to his room.

Later, you worry about physically or emotionally harming your child; your tears overflow as feelings of despair and hopelessness overwhelm you. This is not what you wanted from parenthood. The books about parent-child relationships always show pictures of smiling children cuddling up to a beaming parent. Why hasn't this happened for you? Where did you go wrong?

Perhaps your situation is quite different. It may be that you don't have significant problems with angry or aggressive behavior, because your child is usually loving, cooperative, and obedient at home. His problems revolve around school; he is bright but his grades are dull. He either doesn't complete his assignments or fails to turn them in. The teacher thinks he's lazy.

The symptoms are different, but your feelings of frustration, guilt, and anger are constant. You want your child to succeed, but can't come up with a way to ensure his success. The teacher has suggested various ideas with little progress. Something works for a few days or weeks and then the old pattern returns. You wonder if there isn't something wrong with this kid's brain.

Is there hope? I want to assure you that there is help and hope for children with attention problems. We don't know of any "cure" for this disorder. However, much can be done to restore your faith in yourself and in your ability to care for your child.

Change always has two parts. The first part is *awareness* of the nature of a problem. The balance of this chapter will help you understand the various characteristics of attention disorders, so that you can more clearly identify whether your child has problems of this type.

The second component in bringing about change is appropriate *intervention*. It doesn't do any good to define the existence of a problem and then hope it will get better. There must be specific and relevant procedures that produce changes. The key is to know which interventions will bring about the desired improvements in the behavior of ADHD children. This topic will be the thrust of the remaining chapters. But first we must return to the task of understanding the nature of attention deficits.

Definitions of Attention Disorders

• *History of terms.* Because changes in terminology can be confusing, we will review the history of attention disorders. This will help you see the evolution of thought about the causes of this disorder. Efforts have been made to find a medical basis for problems of attention and overactivity, but the search for causes has been frustrating. New ideas about causation have brought accompanying changes in terms.

One of the earliest descriptions of hyperactive symptoms appeared in 1848 in a children's story written by a German physician about *Fidgety Phil.* The first scientific paper on the subject was written in 1902 by Dr. George Still, who described children who were inattentive, impulsive, and difficult. He referred to these children as having problems with "defects in moral control" and "volitional inhibition." An important feature of Dr. Still's work was his idea that the inattentive and distractible features of these children were not part of normal development. He thought the causes of the problems included heredity, trauma, and learning history. Dr. Still's discussion was helpful, even though he was pessimistic about treatment for these children.

Following a world outbreak of encephalitis in 1917–1918, researchers noted symptoms of restlessness, inattention, over-arousal, and hyperactivity in children who had otherwise recovered from encephalitis. These patterns of behavior were thought to stem from some type of brain injury and were called *post-encephalitic disorders.*

In the 1950s, *psychotropic medications* became a very important part of treatment for institutionalized persons because many of these adults could function in society with the aid of medication. This success brought about a renewed interest in the use of stimulant medications for children with attention difficulties. The primary problem was thought to be hyperactivity. Limited attention span and impulsivity were seen as secondary. The source of hyperactivity was thought to be a brain injury. One of the main terms used during that period was *hyperkinetic impulse disorder.* However, clear evidence of any type of brain damage was still lacking.

Minimal brain dysfunction was the term used in the 1960s. However, much of the research of that decade was focused on the symptoms of the disorder, rather than its causes. By the 1970s, the shift in research resulted in the core problem being seen as *inattention* rather than excessive activity. The idea of brain injury being the cause also fell on hard times.

Further research determined that most children with verifiable brain injuries did not develop hyperactivity. Additionally, hard evidence of structural brain damage was only found in fewer than 5 percent of hyperactive children. Since it could not be shown that there was obvious structural impairment, the term *minimal brain damage* became the diagnostic label of these years. It must have been "minimal" because the researchers couldn't see it. This term persisted, even though there was very little corroborating evidence of central nervous system damage.

A substantial amount of research during the 1970s resulted in the prevailing view that poor attention span and impulse control were of equal importance to hyperactivity. A major shift in views about causation took place during this period. Actual brain damage was thought to have a relatively minor role as the source of these problems. Other brain mechanisms such as underarousal, brain neurotransmitter deficiencies, or neurological immaturity were viewed as possible contributors to the problem. Diet and child-rearing were also seen as important.

In the 1980s study continued, making the topic the most researched problem of childhood. By 1990 most professionals viewed ADHD as a developmentally handicapping condition that was usually chronic in nature. The causes were thought to have a strong biological source and it was believed to be found in children with a hereditary predisposition.[1, 2]

• *Current definition.* As you can see, many terms have been used to describe this condition. It is obvious there has been ambiguity and confusion as researchers have attempted to define the essential features of this condition. Professional debate continues to this day on the exact features of ADHD. However, most authorities agree that the characteristics of inattention, impulsivity, and overactivity must be included.

The most recent attempts to clarify the terminology came through the efforts of the American Psychiatric Association. Their intention was to focus on observable behavior which was unique to each category of problems. The *Diagnostic and Statistical Manual* (3rd edition, Revised) attempts to provide an operational definition of this disorder. The current official term is *attention deficit hyperactivity disorder* (ADHD).[3] As more knowledge is gained, however, this term may be replaced by another.

All children display some of these behaviors at various times in their lives. Therefore, eight or more of these symptoms must be observed over a period of at least six months. To fit this diagnosis, there must be no other evidence of injury or illness, and the symptoms need to start before the child is seven years old. Other emotional problems such as conduct or oppositional disorders must also be ruled out before the ADHD diagnosis will apply.

The next step in developing an awareness of ADHD is to understand the fourteen diagnostic criteria that need to be present to apply the term ADHD. I have put this in a checklist for you to use in comparing the behavior of your child.

Features of Attention Deficit Hyperactivity Disorder based on DSM-III-R[3]

- ☐ Restlessness, fidgets or squirms in seat.
- ☐ Has difficulty remaining seated.
- ☐ Is easily distracted by extraneous stimuli.
- ☐ Has difficulty awaiting turn in game or group situations.
- ☐ Often blurts out answers to questions before they have been completed.
- ☐ Has difficulty following instructions from others.
- ☐ Has difficulty sustaining attention in work or play activities.
- ☐ Often shifts from one uncompleted activity to another.
- ☐ Has difficulty playing quietly.
- ☐ Often talks excessively.
- ☐ Often interrupts or intrudes on others' games.
- ☐ Often does not seem to listen to what is being said.
- ☐ Often loses necessary things.
- ☐ Often engages in physically dangerous activities without considering possible consequences.

What distinguishes the ADHD child from other children is the *number* of different behaviors present, the *length of time* they continue, and the *degree* or intensity to which they are evident. For example, most children will occasionally lose things. To qualify under the ADHD criterion, your child must lose things often and consistently, and across several different situations. The same is true for all fourteen of the criteria.

Remember, this is a beginning awareness. Checking off eight or more of the above characteristics doesn't automatically mean your child has ADHD. There are two major categories of information needed beyond your observations. First, you need to determine if these same behaviors are observed by other persons, such as your child's teacher. You also need to determine if these problems with attention cross several situations, such as church, school, and community. Second, you need the input from a knowledgeable mental health professional such as a psychologist or psychiatrist.

Today there are measurement tools that screen ADHD children. The checklist presented above is very subjective because there is no provision for normative comparisons. We need as much objective data as possible to make reliable decisions about each child. The DSM-III-R list is inadequate by itself to provide an accurate diagnosis. If it is the only factor used in assessment, the incidence will rise to 20 to 25 percent. This means we would come up with too many false positives, too many children who score high on the checklist but who are not really ADHD.

We must use several diagnostic tools and procedures in addition to the DSM-III-R checklist. It is also necessary to consult with a mental health professional such as a psychologist to choose the right selection of procedures to accurately assess your child. Not all ADHD children look and behave the same way, and we must be sensitive to their differences. The type of intervention we choose should be based on the specific needs of the child. We must not blindly treat all attention deficits the same. The answer is to use these diagnostic criteria as part of a comprehensive evaluation which draws on several types of objective assessment instruments. I will give more details about the assessment process in chapter 3.

• *Individual uniqueness and creative potential.* Remember that no ADHD child will have all of the features described. Like snowflakes, no two children are alike. ADHD also has a large collection of traits and behaviors. Some children may have dozens of those traits, while other children will have only a few. Even if two children have an equal number of traits, each set of features can be quite different.

There are positives to ADHD. Many characteristics of these children are quite appropriate and desirable. Their spontaneity, zest, tirelessness, enthusiasm, intensity, curiosity, stimulating brashness, and life-of-the-party energy have their useful moments.

Also, there may be some link between ADHD and giftedness and creativity. These children have rich imaginations and can quickly generate new and different ideas. They can pick up on emotional nuances that other people miss. Many of them can combine ideas in creative ways through art and written forms that no one else has tried. The great need is to bring their problem behaviors under control so that their abilities can be harnessed for good. Perhaps some of the most creative persons in history, such as Thomas Edison and Albert Einstein, may have had ADHD.[4]

Try to remain optimistic and hopeful. Even though the future will hold times of discouragement, the ADHD child and his family can experience joy and success. The purpose of the following chapters is to help you move closer to that goal.

Characteristics of ADHD Children

I will now describe specific ways that children with ADHD act and respond. There are four categories of behavior that most experts report as crucial to identifying the presence of attention disorders.

• Children with ADHD commonly have difficulty with *inattention* and *distractibility.* An ADHD child may have difficulty remaining with a task and focusing his attention, in comparison to other children of the same age. He may daydream or become easily distracted. One minute he is listening to the teacher; then he may switch his focus to the bug on the wall or the bird flying around outside the window. This means he will have difficulty concentrating on schoolwork or anything that requires sustained attention. Completing tasks or following through on instructions will be difficult. This is especially hard if the instructions involve multiple steps. This child gives the impression of not listening, and often loses or forgets things because he is inattentive and distracted.

Just as surprising, and often frustrating to the parent, is the remarkable ability of many ADHD children to pay attention under certain circumstances. An example is watching TV or playing video games. The child may also attend well when he is in the doctor's office or when he is interacting one-on-one with an adult. This variable ability can add to the problem. When parents and teachers see the child attending in one situation, they may conclude that he simply does not try to pay attention at excluded times when he is asked to do chores or listen to instructions.

We assume a child is able to choose to ignore or respond to a stimulus presented to the brain. When a teacher starts talking, for example, a child should consciously shift his concentration from the book he is reading to the teacher's voice. To understand attention disorders, we need to know how much of the attentional choosing is under conscious control and how much is biochemically determined.

In summary, these children have difficulty *beginning* activities, *sustaining* attention until the activity is completed successfully, and *focusing* attention on two stimuli at the same time. Focusing includes tasks such as taking notes in the classroom and watching the teacher write on the board at the same time. Finally, they have trouble being *vigilant* or ready to respond to the next important cue or prompt necessary for instruction or direction.

These children tend to have problems *selecting* and *screening* out the important from the unimportant features of their immediate surroundings in their attempt to attend to a task. ADHD students may also be distracted *internally* by their own thoughts. These difficulties in inattention and distractibility create a dual problem which yields poor and inconsistent performance in many school, home, and social situations.[1]

• The second major characteristic is *overarousal* or *hyperactivity*. Some ADHD children are excessively restless, overactive, and easily aroused. This feature can affect body movement and/or emotions. We will look at these areas separately. It is also important to remember that while hyperactivity used to be the primary descriptive feature in attention disorders, it actually occurs in less than 30 percent of children who have ADHD. Most ADHD children are *not* hyperactive. The terminology has been confusing here. Sometimes *hyperactivity* is used to refer to the entire syndrome of ADHD. Other times the term is intended to describe only the specific characteristic of overarousal. Keep these different uses in mind as you read various books and articles about attention deficit.

Children who are *hyperactive* have difficulty controlling their body movements, especially when they are required to sit still for a long time. This hyperactive aspect of ADHD can range from minor fidgetiness to perpetual motion. A child can have difficulty sitting still in class or can be in constant motion from morning till night. Some hyperactive children also have short and restless sleep patterns.

Because the hyperactive behavior pattern is rarely focused, the child moves from one item to the next with very little purpose. This activity level can rise with increased stimulation in the environment. A trip to the grocery store can be an adventure with a hyperactive child. But a journey to the shopping mall with a stop at the toy store can be an absolute disaster.

• The second component of overarousal is the *emotional variation*. What is obvious here is the extremes of the children's emotions and the quickness with which they go to those extremes. This variation is greater and more intense than in the same features of their peers. Whether happy or sad, their feelings are expressed ever so clearly for everyone to notice. They become frustrated very quickly, often over minor incidents. However, they will forget an upsetting event just as quickly. This can be frustrating to a parent who is still bothered by the outburst and can't understand why the child no longer is agitated. Because of this quick turnaround, the assumption is often made that these children are lacking in conscience. This is usually not true. They have moved on to other thoughts and feelings, and have put the outburst behind them. It's hard to believe sometimes, but it's true.

● The third major characteristic of ADHD is *impulsivity.* These children appear to not think before they act. Due to their concentration problems, they have trouble weighing the consequences of their choices and planning future actions.

In young children, impulsivity may result in frequent injuries. The child often literally leaps before he looks. He may jump off of the back of the couch because it looks like fun, but not have the coordination to land safely. He may also have frequent fights with his friends because of his impulsive words and actions.

This impulsive quality makes these children want to be in charge of all social interactions. As a result they annoy their peers by their attempts to dominate. ADHD children seek to take charge because this dominance allows them to move quickly from one interaction to another so they won't become bored. They may also aggravate others because of their aggressiveness.

In the classroom they may constantly interrupt the teacher, jumping up to answer a question before it is even asked. They are prone to work impulsively on paper, jotting down answers without thinking problems through or reading the complete question.

When you reason one-to-one with children who have attention deficit, they can often logically analyze the consequences of their actions. But put them back in a group and they seem to be overwhelmed and again act first and think later.

A major characteristic of an ADHD child is his trouble following rule-governed behavior. He may know the rule and be able to explain it to you. But ten minutes later, when the parent is not looking, that same child is unable to control his behavior. The need for immediate gratification and an inability to stop and think, results in repeated offenses. This leads to more impetuous, nonthinking behavior. And from all appearances, the child does not learn from his experience. The parent may often label this behavior as willfully disobedient, inconsiderate, and oppositional. This child is frustrating because of his inability to benefit from experience.

One way to understand the essence of ADHD is to imagine *a thick barrier.* This barrier stands firmly between the child and the attempts of the outside world to control his behavior. The rewards, punishments, and consequences that usually make it through the child's skull and influence behavior seem to bounce off the ADHD child's thick barrier. It is like a giant callus that overlays the brain, keeping instructions and consequences out. Even when the message gets through, its impact doesn't last for very long.[6]

A leading researcher and proponent of the thick-barrier hypothesis is Dr. Russell Barkley. He summarizes the core problems in the following way. The *primary deficits* of ADHD children are:[6, 2]

–Inability to cope with routine rules.
–Inability to sustain appropriate behavior in the absence of clear, frequent, and immediate consequences.
–Effects of rewards and punishments wear off quickly.

These deficits concern the ADHD child's inherent difficulties in being appropriately regulated by his environment. An ADHD child falters when confronted by rules. He has problems completing tasks unless there are very clear limits and immediate consequences to the behavior. Reinforcements must also be interesting and meaningful to have any effect. This last characteristic takes us to the next unique feature.

● Most children with attention deficits have *difficulty with rewards.* ADHD children have problems working toward a long-term goal. They often want brief, repeated payoffs, rather than a single, delayed reward. They want what they want right away and are less patient than we would expect children of that age to be. Even with repeated rewards, ADHD children do not respond as well as other children to incentive systems. They often learn to work to avoid aversive or negative consequences (negative reinforcement), rather than to earn positive consequences. Also, once the reward system and structure is removed, the ADHD child is more likely to regress.

Punishments also seem to have limited effect on the child's behavior. A scolding might keep a non-ADHD child well be haved for most of a day. It will usually work on the ADHD child only for a few minutes before the misbehavior resumes.

Developmental Profile of ADHD

Now we will look at ADHD characteristics from a developmental perspective. The major categories of inattention, overarousal, impulsivity, and difficulty with rewards will be present at each age. This discussion will help identify how these major symptoms present themselves at each of the developmental stages.

• *Preschool children.* At some point most parents will describe their preschooler as inattentive and overactive. Eventually these qualities will level out. As a result, these descriptions alone will not help identify young ADHD children. It is recommended that any of the symptoms of ADHD have at least a one-year duration before being considered a stable condition.

Young children with a durable pattern of ADHD are restless, always on the go, acting as if driven by a motor. They can be like a walking tornado — they move into a room pulling toys off shelves, dumping out baskets of crayons, and knocking over the dolls and blocks. If an object is not nailed down, it will be picked up or pushed over. They frequently climb on and get into things. They are more likely to have injuries as a result of their overactive, inattentive, and fearless behavior. They are forever getting hurt but never learning from the experience. They don't know why they jump out of open windows. It just seems like a good idea at the time.

Child-proofing your home is a good idea to help prevent accidents and injuries. It also is necessary to protect family valuables, such as your grandmother's Tiffany lamp, from the vigorous and destructive pattern of play often seen in these children. They are persistent in their wants, demanding of attention, and have an insatiable curiosity about the world.

It is at this preschool stage that we begin to see the child's ability to focus and concentrate is impaired. He may watch TV for five minutes, get distracted, and color for five minutes. Then he sees a friend outside and wants to run out and play, even though it is bedtime and his mother has just told him to get in the bathtub.

In a one-on-one situation, the child can sustain attention for longer periods, although there will still be a lack of ability in this area. Also, exposure to a group usually results in more distractibility and higher activity levels.

Sometimes, even in a group, an ADHD preschool child will focus on an activity by blocking out the rest of the world. Then he may concentrate for long periods watching a television program, digging in the sand, or playing with Legos. When a child's focus is locked on an activity, it can be difficult to distract him. You may need to go to the child and touch him on the shoulder in order to get his attention. This will work much better than yelling. While focusing on his program, he really doesn't see or hear what is going on around him. It is frustrating to work with a child when you think he is ignoring you. You need to remember that the child with an attention deficit has to tune everything else out in order to concentrate. He isn't making a conscious choice to ignore you—he probably doesn't hear you at all. The child may not have this tuning-out ability all the time, and it usually doesn't happen in a group setting. You do need to recognize this "blocking out" process does occur from time to time, and then treat your child with understanding.[5]

All of this presents a major challenge to the parents. Patterns of family disruption are established quite early. Negative cycles of tell-remind-yell-spank become established. It becomes easy to see the child as a negative influence on the whole family.

Some ADHD preschoolers also have excessive moodiness, quickness to anger, and low adaptability. Temper tantrums are common for all preschoolers, but the frequency and intensity is greater in ADHD children. Also, some ADHD preschool children may show rhythmic patterns such as head-banging or rocking. This may first show up in their crib or bed, but it can also happen while they are playing or trying to focus.

Stomach problems are common in ADHD children. Lack of

coordination in large or small muscle group activities is also noticeable. They will produce sloppy or messy seatwork at preschool, Sunday School, or kindergarten.

There is a great deal of off-task behavior. The child will wander away from his seat or table at school. While the teacher is instructing other children on a certain task, this child will be doing something else. He requires greater amounts of adult attention and supervision than do most other preschool children.

Preschool ADHD children begin a pattern of intrusiveness. They bother others by talking to them, touching them, or intruding on their projects and play. They also seek attention through inappropriate or excessive ways such as making animal noises, teasing, or clowning.

At times these children do slow down enough to interact, and then we find they can be very loving and caring. We see that they want very much to please and have a hard time understanding why everyone is so frustrated with them. When they break something in their relentless pursuit of activity, they truly are remorseful. They fail to learn from these experiences, though, and as other acts of aggression increase, they begin to alienate their peers and teachers.

● *School-age children.* Once ADHD children enter school, a major social burden is placed upon them that will last for at least the next twelve years. School makes the greatest demands on their areas of disability and can create a large amount of distress for the child and his family. The abilities to sit still, attend, listen, obey, inhibit impulsive behavior, cooperate, organize actions, and be pleasant with other children are essential to negotiating a successful school career. These skills go beyond the cognitive and achievement skills needed to master the curriculum itself. And if there are any types of learning disabilities in addition to ADHD, the burden is multiplied. Because of these demands, identification of ADHD often takes place after entry into the full-time classroom.

The school may raise the issue of retaining the child in either kindergarten or first grade because of immature behavior and/or low academic achievement. Homework requirements become a focus of concern because of the ADHD child's inability to complete them or turn them in. Daydreaming, talking out, and out-of-seat behavior are frequently reported by the teachers of ADHD elementary students.

It is common to hear a parent complain that their perfectly bright child can get all of his spelling words the night before the test. But at exam time the ADHD child acts as though he'd been raised in Madagascar and had never seen an English spelling list in his life. The student sincerely wants to do his best, but the schoolwork doesn't improve.

This child will be listening to the teacher one minute; then a classmate will sneeze or drop a pencil and his attention will be lost. Then he can't redirect himself back to the original focus. His distractibility makes it hard to complete an assignment. He starts out with a strong effort, but loses his train of thought and ends up on a whole different track. He may not even get past putting a heading on the paper before he completely forgets the assigned task.

Free flight of ideas is a constant problem for young school children with attention deficit. Their minds may wander so extensively that they actually spend a large portion of their school day in a world of imagination. While they think about birthday parties and baseball games, they look like they are concentrating on what the teacher is saying. In reality, their minds are miles away.

Impulsivity can seriously affect schoolwork. The ADHD child may not take the time to think through what he is doing in regard to a written assignment. He may work quickly and carelessly, making frequent spelling errors by leaving out letters. The child may make many mistakes on simple math problems by putting numbers in the wrong columns or using an incorrect procedure, such as subtracting instead of adding.

Disorganization is very common in the ADHD student. Inevitably, the child will bring home the wrong book or forget the dentist appointment right after school. He will fail to turn in the homework he spent an hour completing with his parents the night before. The same applies to chores around the home. The child with attention deficit fully intends to cut the lawn. He just got distracted by the neighborhood football game and forgot to finish the lawn—leaving the lawn mower, rake, and garbage bags right in the middle of the yard. The end result is that children with ADHD need more supervision and assistance with daily chores and self-help activities such as dressing and bathing.

The ADHD child is forgetful when it comes to his belongings. He continually misplaces articles of clothing, shoes, toys, and books. Parents may have a terrible time getting the child off to school on time with matching shoes and socks, jacket, lunch, textbooks, and homework—he will have no idea where the missing items are. Homework papers will turn up in the clothes hamper, and the lost lunch is eventually found in the toy box.

Social rejection results. Even when an ADHD child displays appropriate behavior toward others, it may be at such a high rate or intensity that it elicits rejection. Vocal noisiness, and a tendency to touch and manipulate objects more than is normal for this age, combine to make the ADHD child overwhelming, intrusive, and aversive to others. It is common to find these children developing feelings of low self-esteem about school and peers. Yet many will blame their problems on their teachers, classmates, or parents because of their limited self-awareness. As they grow, temper tantrums will decline, as happens with most children, but ADHD children will still have more temper outbursts than non-ADHD children.

Relationships with siblings may be filled with tension and conflict. Some brothers and sisters will develop resentment over the greater burden they often carry compared to their hyperactive siblings. They may also become jealous over the amount of time an ADHD brother or sister demands from their parents.

Most children become active in extracurricular community activities such as sports teams, clubs, scouts, and church groups. ADHD children may find themselves barely tolerated or even rejected. Parents then have to come to the rescue, explain or apologize to leaders, and try to negotiate the child's reentry into the group.[2]

Many of these attention-deficit characteristics sound like

normal childhood traits. Most children are distractible, forgetful, impulsive, and moody at times. All children daydream occasionally and have trouble concentrating on reading material or the words of a speaker. What makes these characteristics significant is their severity and persistence. The frequency with which these features present themselves, and the degree to which they interfere with adequate functioning, reflect their importance in distinguishing the child who has attention deficit.

Ten Things to Do with a Pencil — If You're ADHD

1. Blow it across the desk.
2. Fly it through the air.
3. Hold it high in the air and drop it.
4. Stick it in the screws of the chair.
5. Thread it through your belt loops.
6. Pick the threads of your socks.
7. Roll it inside your desk.
8. Poke your neighbor.
9. Sharpen it—resharpen it.
10. Lose it.[9]

• *Adolescents.* Even under "normal" circumstances, adolescence is a challenging developmental period for families. The teenager is undergoing major physiological, cognitive, behavioral, and emotional changes. However, the normal problems of this phase are magnified greatly for the individual with ADHD. This happens because the features of attention deficit interfere with successfully mastering the developmental tasks of adolescence. The emerging issues of independence, identity, peer group acceptance, dating, and appearance erupt as new sources of demands and distress with which the ADHD adolescent and his family must cope. As a result, ADHD teens encounter academic failure, social isolation, diminished hopes about future success, depression, and low self-esteem. They also become embroiled in many unpleasant conflicts with their families. Many of the problems relate to noncompliance around the house and to school-related issues such as homework.

Many studies have dispelled the notion that ADHD is typically outgrown by the adolescent years. Most children diagnosed as hyperactive in childhood continue to display their symptoms to a significant degree in adolescence and young adulthood. The symptoms of ADHD that present themselves in adolescents are the very same as found in childhood. The fourteen characteristics in the DSM-III-R list continue to apply, although they may be difficult to separate from normal features of adolescence such as impulsiveness and moodiness.[2]

There may be two distinct groups of ADHD adolescents. The first is the student who has some type of learning disability along with their attention deficit. Children with a mild form of attention deficit, but who are well motivated and who are receiving help for their learning problems, can sometimes overcome their concentration problems without need for additional help. They may never be identified as ADHD because they were thought to have only learning problems that needed attention. However, if the learning disability is accompanied by ADHD, the increasing demands of junior high and high school may overload the coping or compensation system the child was using to offset either problem. The combination of ADHD and learning disabilities will prove too much, and a dramatic deterioration in academic performance will result.

The second type of adolescent diagnosed with attention deficit has above-average intelligence and a very involved, motivated family. In the early years of school, there might have been indicators of ADHD, usually without hyperactivity. But because the child had the skills to cope, the problem did not become serious enough for recognition until he hit secondary school. Because he was bright, it took longer for his coping techniques to be overwhelmed.

Closely related is the child with some ADHD features who had a very supportive school and home environment which provided needed assistance along the way. Tutoring help, private school, or parental assistance with homework may have carried the student until the increased demands of high school overcame the ability of the student and his family to compensate.

The diagnosis of attention deficit in older students can come as a tremendous relief and can help explain why school has been so difficult. I have had students who came to me during their high school years feeling stupid and depressed. They knew they were capable of doing most of the work and couldn't understand why the organization, memory work, or note-taking was so difficult. Often a comprehensive assessment helped to separate any learning disabilities from ADHD symptoms and we could systematically work on the respective problems. Some of these students have come back with enthusiastic thankfulness for determining they were not stupid and for pointing the way to dealing with their problems.

• *Adults.* There are currently no consensus criteria for making the diagnosis of ADHD in adults. Some efforts have been made to adapt the earlier DSM-III-R criteria to adult diagnosis. Other researchers are working on a new set of descriptions for inattention and hyperactive/impulsive behavior. Following are the draft set of symptom descriptions for each of these categories.[2]

Inattentive:
–Trouble directing and sustaining attention (conversations, lectures, reading, instructions, driving).
–Difficulty completing projects, lacks stick-to-it-tiveness.
–Easily overwhelmed by task of daily living (managing money, paying bills, applying for college, etc.).
–Trouble maintaining an organized living/work place.
–Inconsistent work performance.
–Lacks attention to detail.

Hyperactive/Impulsive
–Makes decisions impulsively and doesn't anticipate consequences.
–Difficulty delaying gratification; seeks out stimulation.
–Restless, fidgety.
–Makes statements without considering their impact.

–Impatient, easily frustrated.

–Traffic violations (speeding, running stop signs).

These descriptions are tentative for adults with ADHD, but will give you an idea of how the previously described symptoms of childhood can present themselves in the adult context.

Questions Often Asked about ADHD

1. Is it true that boys have ADHD more often than girls?

Some studies have shown boys are at least three times more likely to have ADHD than girls. Other research suggests the incidence is six times higher in boys than girls.

Other data indicates that when more precise measures of attention are used, the incidence may be more equal. Girls tend to display their ADHD more through attention deficits than through problems with impulsivity and aggression. Girls are often seen as "daydreamers" rather than hyperactive. They tend to have fewer problems with outward conduct, so aren't referred as often. Thus, girls may be seriously under-diagnosed.[6]

No one is sure why ADHD appears to be more common in boys. We do know that boys seem to be more at risk in developing almost any childhood behavioral or emotional problem. For example, three or four times as many boys as girls are referred for reading problems. Current thoughts about ADHD is that it may be a sex-linked predisposition which causes the condition to show up more frequently in males. More research is needed to complete the explanation. We also need to make sure our definition of ADHD does not bias our search in the direction of overactivity and leave out the less active girls.

2. Do children with ADHD also have other significant problems?

In addition to problems with inattention, impulsivity, over-arousal, and rule-governed behavior, the ADHD child can have various other conditions. For example, 25 to 35 percent of ADHD children may also have some type of learning disability. A child with a learning disability shows a significant discrepancy between his potential and actual academic performance; he is hampered by a specific deficiency in one or more modalities of learning. This means he not only finds it hard to pay attention in the classroom but also finds it difficult to process certain types of information given by the teacher even when he is paying attention. In such cases, the ADHD student is in double trouble, and it is easy to see why he can quickly become turned off to school.[7]

Children with ADHD have a higher likelihood of sleeping problems than normal children. They often have more trouble getting to sleep as well as frequent night wakings. As a result many parents report these children often appear to be still tired when they get up in the mornings.

Various conduct problems are also common in ADHD youngsters. Stubbornness, defiance, or refusal to obey, temper tantrums, and verbal hostility are evident in many of these children. In some cases severe forms of lying, stealing, truancy, and physical aggression are present.

Because of these various accompanying or coexistent problems, it is important to involve a professional, who will help you differentiate ADHD from other categories, such as conduct or oppositional disorder, and develop appropriate intervention strategies.

3. Is there any difference in the real intentions of an ADHD child and other children?

One way to differentiate between the ADHD child and the child who looks hyperactive but is not is the "can't versus won't" dimension. The ADHD child can intentionally be disobedient. Yet he often has trouble with self-control, sustained attention, and organization, even when he wants to do well. You have a sense that sometimes the ADHD child cannot pay attention or follow the rules, in spite of his best efforts.

To illustrate, I would like to share a short essay written by an ADHD student. The essay was assigned after an act of disobedience. (It was one of many such failures.) The topic was "Following Rules" and I think this boy's statements show how he really wants to be obedient but often fails (I corrected his spelling to make it easier to get his poignant message.)

It's good to follow the rules because if you don't you

could get hurt, die, break a bone, or have a bad injury. I should follow the rules too. I try to, but it's hard for me because I'm too hyper. If you don't follow the rules, you will get a lot of referrals. Too many referrals means suspension from school. If you don't follow the rules you'll end up like me, a low-down scumbucket. I am a very bad kid in school.

I like school. The only problem is I always have trouble. I'll do anything if you don't tell my mom about this. Also if you don't follow the rules, you'll never grow up right and nobody will like you. You might become a robber and steal jewelry. You'll be rich but it was stupid of you to steal in the first place. You never learn anything if you don't follow the rules. I barely ever follow the rules. I never learn anything.

If you don't follow the rules, when you're grown up you might turn out like a bum. And you'll never ever be smart unless you go back to school and start from the third grade. I get bad grades because I don't follow the rules that much. Always follow the rules and you'll never ever be a bad person.

You get the feeling from this boy's letter that he really wants to follow the rules and do well in school. At the same time he is very discouraged because he can't do a better job.

In contrast, the disobedient child who is not ADHD often shows the capacity for self-control. You get the feeling from this child that he chooses, either consciously or otherwise, to resist following the rules. If you know this capable but noncompliant child well enough, you begin to get a sense of willfulness or "won't" that tells you the capability to behave correctly is there. However, the child chooses otherwise.

In the chapters on various forms of intervention, I will highlight the importance of *discerning between noncompliance and incompetence*. Sometimes, with an ADHD child, expecting him to follow certain rules consistently is similar to asking a blind person to read the evening newspaper. The difference is that a blind person will consistently be unable to see, while an ADHD child can sometimes follow the rules and sometimes not. Life isn't easy for the ADHD child or for his parents.

4. Do ADHD children grow out of their problem?

The common belief used to be that ADHD was an early childhood problem, and that once the child became a teenager, ADHD went away. This was because we used to focus exclusively on the child's overactivity, which does tend to lessen dramatically as the child grows older. However, we now know that the inattentiveness and impulsiveness of children with ADHD do not simply disappear with time. Although the attention span can improve as the child matures, teenagers with ADHD continue to experience more problems in these areas than do their peers.

The good news is that recent research indicates 35 to 50 percent of children with ADHD do fairly well as adults. And there is increasing evidence that with early identification and appropriate treatment, children with ADHD can grow up to be responsible, productive, and happy adults.[3, 2]

This concludes our general discussion of the definition and nature of ADHD. You should have a pretty good idea of the various features of attention deficits. These characteristics include: inattention, impulsivity, overactivity, and difficulty with rule-governed behavior. You may also have some strong impressions about whether your child has ADHD, but don't make any final judgments yet. You need more information. In the next chapter we will look at the causes of ADHD. This will include a discussion of several false beliefs about parental and environmental influences. I think you will find it helpful.

References

1. Goldstein, S., and Goldstein, M., *Managing Attention Disorders in Children* (New York: John Wiley & Sons, 1990).

2. Barkley, R.A., *Attention-Deficit Hyperactivity Disorder: A Handbook for Diagnosis and Treatment* (New York: The Guilford Press, 1990).

3. American Psychiatric Association, *Diagnostic and Statistical Manual of Mental Disorders,* 3rd edition—revised (Wash-

ington, D.C.:1987).

4. Taylor, J.F., *Helping Your Hyperactive Child* (Rocklin, California: Prima Publishing & Communications, 1990).

5. Moss, R.A., *Why Johnny Can't Concentrate: Coping with Attention-Deficit Problems* (New York: Bantam Books, 1990).

6. Gordon, M., *ADHD/Hyperactivity: A Consumer's Guide* (DeWitt, New York: GSI Publications, 1991).

7. Barkley, R.A., *Attention-Deficit Hyperactivity Disorder: A Clinical Workbook* (New York: The Guilford Press, 1991).

8. Greenberg, G.S., and Horn, W.F., *Attention-Deficit Hyperactivity Disorder: Questions & Answers for Parents* (Champaign, Illinois: Research Press, 1991).

9. Maxey, Debra W., *How to Own and Operate an Attention-Deficit Kid* (Roanoke, Virginia: HyperActive Attention Deficit [HAAD], P.O. Box 20563, Roanoke, VA 24018, 1989).

ChAPTER TWO

WHY IS MY CHILD HYPERACTIVE?
Causes and Sources
of ADHD

Why does my child have these problems?"
      "Is his ADHD caused by something we did as parents?"

"Could this have been prevented?"

As you toss in your sleep at night, you may have wondered about the causes of your child's attention disorders. In this chapter, I will give you the best answers scientific research has been able to provide about the origins of these problems. The most accurate general statement I can make is that we don't really know for sure what causes ADHD. There are many pet theories, some more promising than others. I'll give a summary of each of the main areas of exploration.

ADHD continues to be one of the most thoroughly researched conditions of childhood. Yet the exact causes are still not known. Neurochemical abnormalities which might underlie this disorder are difficult to document. The research appears to be moving toward a consensus that ADHD has a biological base. The data points to a genetically endowed predisposition, along with a common neurological mechanism. In other words, many ADHD children seem to arrive in the world with temperaments that leave them difficult to manage. Part of the basis for this predisposition may be inherited. Very often I will hear parents describe their child as "a chip off the old block," or say, "I acted the same way when I was a kid." They may tell me about relatives who appeared to have a history of inattentive and overactive behavior. All of this suggests a genetic basis for the problem. I'll describe some of the details shortly.

Environmental conditions may play a role also. However, factors like diet show up on an individual basis, rather than in large numbers. For example, sugar has not been shown to be a consistent source of overactive behavior. Yet there definitely are a few children who have dramatic negative reactions to excessive sugar in their diet.

Parenting and ADHD

The symptoms of ADHD are *not* externally created by parents. It is extremely important for you as a parent not to blame yourself. You did not cause your child's attention problems through faulty discipline. It is true that parental frustration and negative reactions toward your child can aggravate the problem. Your guilt, anger, and resentment can contaminate the relationship with your child and interfere with effective treatment. Your behavior can have a substantial effect on your child in both positive and negative ways, but your actions alone did not create ADHD in your child. Negative home environments such as family dysfunction, divorce, abuse, and faulty parenting can certainly produce behavior patterns that resemble ADHD. And, as we have seen, children with ADHD often have other problems. That is one reason why an accurate diagnosis is needed. More about that in the next chapter. For now, realize your influence as a parent is indeed crucial to the overall emotional health of your child. A nurturing home with clear and consistent structure is crucial to the treatment of ADHD children. However, your actions did not bring about attention deficit.

Theories about the cause of ADHD

Let's look at some of the ideas that have been propagated to explain the causes of ADHD. I will first describe some factors which appear to play a minor role in the origin of attention deficit and hyperactivity.

● *Brain injury* was one of the first causal theories. ADHD was thought to occur as a result of brain infections, trauma, or other injuries or complications taking place during pregnancy or delivery. Brain damage can result in symptoms of hyperactivity, inattentiveness, and impulsivity. It was the association of these symptoms with brain injury and brain infection that led to the disorder being called *minimal brain damage*. Because of this association, inattention and hyperactivity were thought to be signs that brain damage had occurred. Researchers then attempted to identify the possible causes of brain damage.

One such source is brain damage that may occur as a result of an *infection* in the mother or from *drugs* taken by the mother. The latter include prescription drugs as well as substances such as alcohol and cocaine. Babies born with fetal alcohol syndrome are known to suffer from severe behavioral problems which can include hyperactivity. Recent data collected from maternity hospitals show that 375,000 babies are born each year with drugs in their systems. It is estimated that 20 percent of all newborns have been exposed to drugs in the womb. The National Institute on Drug Abuse estimates that 4.5 percent of all newborns are exposed to cocaine in the womb.[1]

A study was done of 1,900 infants born with cocaine in their systems at New York City's Harlem Hospital. Of these babies, over one-third were premature, and 15 percent had lifetime handicaps, such as mental retardation, cerebral palsy, or blindness due to strokes in the womb. Nearly all the remaining children had less serious afflictions that emerged later, including hyperactivity, impaired motor skills, and delays in language use.[1]

Some of these children have symptoms of ADHD, but the connection is still not clear. More studies are needed to clarify the exact influence of drugs and toxins on infants.

So far, the reviews of the evidence suggest that fewer than 5 percent of ADHD children have hard neurological findings indicative of actual brain damage.[2]

• *Birth injury.* This has long been suspected to be a major cause of ADHD and other neurological problems of childhood. Researchers studied 66,000 pregnancies in the Collaborative Perinatal Project, keeping detailed records of all aspects of pregnancy, labor, and delivery. Psychological, neurological, and medical follow-up examinations were conducted during the child's development after birth. The Apgar score was used to measure the health of the infant. This consists of a five-part rating system of a newborn based on movement, tone, color, respiratory effort, and heart rate. The Apgar score did not correlate with subsequent development of ADHD symptoms. This indicates that on an individual basis, a difficult pregnancy or delivery is not sufficient to establish birth injury as the cause of ADHD.[3]

While certain types of trauma, infection, or disease of the central brain may contribute to the development of ADHD, these causes account for very few ADHD children.

• Other researchers have speculated that ADHD may be due to some type of *delayed brain maturation.* This idea would appear to have merit, given the immature social behavior of ADHD children. There are also frequent findings of maturational delay on neurological exams, and there is a similarity between the ADHD child's deficits in attention, impulse control, and self-regulation with that of younger normal children. At this time, there is no direct neurological evidence available to support this theory, so it remains hypothetical.

• The possibility of *lead poisoning* has also been examined. Lead is a strong neurotoxin that can be found in the peeling and chipping paint of older homes. It was also found in the solder used in years past to weld water pipes. Gasolines containing lead have contributed to high levels of airborne lead in some polluted areas.

There is evidence to indicate that lead in the body can be associated with hyperactivity and inattention in a general population. Some studies have measured the amount of lead in the blood, hair, or the dentine of children's teeth. When teachers were asked to rate the level of hyperactivity and inattention in those same children, some studies did show significant relationships between higher lead levels and attention ratings. Other studies have indicated a low correlation between lead blood levels and hyperactivity. The problem is that ADHD children often show little or no increase in their body lead indicators. The present opinion is that lead may be a contributor to attention and learning problems in some children. However, it is unlikely to be a major cause of ADHD, even though it is a major health problem for the public at large.[4, 5]

• *Food Additives.* Additives such as salicylates, food dyes, and preservatives were highly publicized causes of ADHD during the 1970s and early 1980s. In 1974 Dr. Benjamin Feingold, a pediatric allergist, claimed that over half of all hyperactivity was caused by artificial colors and flavors. Dr. Feingold suspected the apparent increase in hyperactivity over the past several decades coincided with increased use of artificial flavors, colors, and preservatives in our food supply. It was the artificial colors which he most suspected because they have a certain chemical similarity to substances known to produce allergic responses.

Dr. Feingold then proposed a complex diet to eliminate these substances, and cited anecdotal evidence to support his theory. He never conducted a controlled study of the problem. However, a substantial amount of research since that time has been unable to support these claims. A few preschool children may have shown a small increase in activity or inattentiveness when consuming these additives. But no evidence has been presented that shows normal children can acquire ADHD symptoms by consuming such substances. Nor has it been shown that ADHD children are made worse by them. Any improvement in behavior when a diet was introduced was primarily a placebo effect. Most early formal studies did not show clear evidence implicating artificial salicylates and food additives as a substantial cause of ADHD.[6]

The artificial sweetener *aspartame* (trade names "Equal" and "NutraSweet") has also come under scrutiny as a possible cause of ADHD. From a theoretical standpoint, aspartame does look like a suspicious candidate. It is made up of two amino acids, phenylalanine and aspartic acid, that play important roles in the brain's synthesis of neurotransmitters. Aspartame was extensively studied for cancer-causing potential before it was approved by the Food and Drug Administration. However, it was not researched for its effects on behavior.

A few children appear to suffer extreme reactions to aspartame, including behavior problems, seizures, and headaches. In the studies reported so far, no consistent problems or connection to attention deficits have been identified. Some people may be especially sensitive to aspartame, but the effects otherwise appear to be subtle. The recommendation at this time is to observe your child closely for reactions and restrict his diet if your observations suggest any problems.

It may be prudent to avoid all such products as much as possible. The possibilities of harm are too great to take a risk with something like aspartame which has no nutritional value. At the same time, parents need to teach their children how to monitor their reactions to foods. Children must learn that it is important to manage their diet as it relates to mental health, in the same way it is necessary to brush their teeth and practice good hygiene.

• In spite of the early lack of results, recent studies have been more positive about diet and *food intolerances.* For example, investigators have eliminated multiple food offenders, instead of single foods, with some success. They have eliminated not only artificial colors and flavors, but also chocolate, monosodium glutamate, preservatives, caffeine, and many substances that families reported might affect their specific child. The suggested diet was also low in simple sugars and was even milk-free if the family reported a history of possible problems with cow's milk. More than half of the children were reported to improve on the diet, but not on the placebo. The authors believed their diet had a stronger effect than previous studies because they eliminated many offending agents, not just one. Only further research will determine if this approach has any relevance to the daily lives of most ADHD children.[7]

Toxic environmental influences must have some kind of effect on ADHD children. Many children with ADHD and/or learning problems seem to have numerous *allergies*. For example, 94 percent of ADHD children have had three or more ear infections, compared to a 50 percent incidence for normal children; 69 percent of ADHD children have had ten or more ear infections compared to only 20 percent of normal children who have had that many infections.[8] This strongly suggests some type of allergy relationship.

Some children definitely have food intolerances. Dairy products, for example, are frequent offenders. We don't know how all of this fits together in relation to attention deficit. Foods significantly affect the way children behave, learn, and feel. However, it is important to resist the temptation to jump to conclusions without careful safeguards and controlled studies.

It is essential to keep a balance between healthy skepticism and openmindedness when it comes to suspecting foods for the aberrant behavior of children. We need additional rigorous scientific investigation to help us understand these possible connections. An example is Dr. Conners' recent work which suggests a link between *when* certain foods are eaten and the effect on behavior. Sugar and carbohydrates eaten alone for breakfast can cause problems. But these same foods can be tolerated if eaten with protein.[9] I guess you can have a cinnamon roll for breakfast, but you need to eat a lean steak or beans or egg along with it to avoid becoming a Fidgety Phil.

• *Refined sugar.* Sugar has also been a popular explanation for ADHD. Anecdotes regarding sugar and hyperactivity appeared in the scientific literature as early as 1929. It is legitimate to question the effects of sugar in our diet, since the average person in the United States consumes almost 132 pounds of sugar per year. Some would argue that sugar acts like a stimulant to speed us up. Others would say it makes us depressed. So we have theories which range from a "buzz effect" to "sugar blues."

Despite widespread attention by the general public about the negative effects of sugar, there have been few or no scientific studies actually conducted by those who propose to eliminate sugar. Their evidence is mostly anecdotal. In the controlled studies of sugar which have been conducted over the years, researchers have approached the topic in two ways. One is to try to correlate dietary sugar intake with behavior. The second is to give large amounts of sugar to children and observe their reactions. These studies have generally shown no negative outcome across groups of children. Some individual children certainly react with ADHD symptoms with ingestion of refined sugar and/or other additives, but there has been no documented effect for significant numbers of children. While controlled studies have failed to prove a direct sugar connection, the number of anecdotes from parents that suggest it are too numerous to discount.

Rather than ask, "Is sugar bad for children?" researchers such as Dr. Keith Conners have suggested it may be better to ask, "Under what circumstances is sugar beneficial or harmful?" Sugar can be either negative or positive for children, depending on their age, diet, and biology. There is a good possibility that a child's changing brain may leave him vulnerable to sugar and carbohydrates at certain ages. But there may be a vulnerability to either too little or too much. Protein seems to have an important protective role when sugars or other carbohydrates are eaten. This argues for generous amounts of protein in a child's diet. No findings justify eliminating sugar from a child's diet; nor should the desirable features of protein mean that a child should load up on meat, cheese, or fish exclusively. The principle to follow is balance. Carbohydrates, including sugar, are essential ingredients in a normal diet. A varied, well-balanced diet is still the best protection against adverse physical and mental consequences related to food. A nutritionist, dietician, or knowledgeable physician can help you tailor a program for the needs of your child.[9]

• *Medical illness.* Illness can cause poor attention in many nonspecific ways. There is disagreement about whether attention problems that emerge from illness should even be called ADHD. Specific illnesses which have been linked to ADHD symptoms include iron deficiency, anemia, hyperthyroidism, pinworms, rheumatic chorea, hypoglycemia, and petit mal epilepsy. These are uncommon causes for ADHD, but they should be considered in any complete medical evaluation.

• *Medications.* Medicine taken to treat other illnesses can also trigger ADHD symptoms. An example is anticonvulsants such as Phenobarbital and Dilantin®, and medications which tend to be sedating and can reduce attentiveness and concentration. Also, various medications given to treat asthma, colds, or allergies can act as stimulants.

It is unlikely that these medications are a major cause of ADHD. However, if your child is taking medication for epilepsy, for example, you should be alert to the possibility of the anticonvulsants worsening a preexisting condition. Likewise, medications taken for an allergy can produce inattention, and you should be aware of that connection.

Hereditary and Neurological Factors
Heredity is the single factor shown to be a common denominator among ADHD children. Children with ADHD are four times more likely to have siblings and parents with ADHD than are normal children. Also, children with ADHD raised by an adoptive family are four times more likely to have ADHD in their natural parents than adopted children without ADHD.

A fairly recent study evaluated the heritability of hyperactivity among a large group of identical and fraternal twins. The results showed that if one identical twin develops ADHD, the other one carries a significantly increased risk of developing attention deficit. The authors concluded that genetic factors play a significant role in this disorder.

Let's take a brief look at some aspects of brain function which relate to attention disorders. *Thinking functions* of the brain are localized within the cerebral hemisphere. When a child reads a math problem, information is transmitted from the eyes through the visual pathways to a part of the brain called the occipital lobes. This visual image has no meaning until it is coordinated with the parietal lobe region. The child now is able to comprehend the nature of the question and the answer is prepared. Information is then sent to the frontal region of the brain where the response is translated into a verbal or written answer. If a child has problems with attention and distractibility, we would expect this frontal region of the brain to at least be partially involved. Some studies in recent years have begun to clarify the dynamics of how ADHD might be related to problems with this part of the brain.

One of the landmark studies traced ADHD to a specific metabolic abnormality in the brain. In this study researchers used a sophisticated brain-imaging technique known as positron-emission tomography (PET), and scanned to measure sugar metabolism in the brain cells of adults who had been hyperactive since childhood and had at least one child with the same problem. The results were striking. The overall brain metabolism was 8 percent lower in hyperactive subjects than in a control group; the largest differences were found in two regions of the brain — the premotor cortex and the superior prefrontal cortex. These are parts of the brain known to be involved in regulating attention and motor control. It was not clear what causes these metabolic differences, but the link between brain chemistry and behavior was more clearly established.[13]

Thus far I have described how cognitive functioning can be identified with specific locations in the brain. However, no such localization seems to exist for *attention deficit*. There is no neurological marker presently understood for ADHD; no single part of the brain is underdeveloped or injured, as far as we know. No particular part of the brain, when removed, produces ADHD symptoms. This means *ADHD is more of a system problem than a component dysfunction.* It might be analogous to the brake fluid in your car's braking system. The mechanical components of the brake system work okay, but the fluid itself is ether absent or decomposed to the point that it can't send the message from your brake pedal to the wheels. Consequently, the wheels don't get the information telling them to slow down. As a result, the car runs right through a stop sign, ending up in a collision.

What causes the system to fail? The following description is the best opinion we have at this time. The brain-stem centers contain the cell bodies which produce chemicals such as norepinephrine, serotonin, and dopamine. These chemicals are then sent through the axons to all areas of the brain. At this time, research suggests the dysfunction of the *dopamine system* is an important contribution to ADHD.

Let's picture how the brain functions in regard to attention, and how the dopamine system fits into that picture. When a brain cell is stimulated, it releases a neurotransmitter that carries the message to the next cell. The neurotransmitter attaches itself to the cell, causing that cell to be stimulated. Then another messenger is released. It's kind of like playing tag. The person who is "it" runs and touches the first person he can catch. That second person becomes "it" and runs to catch somebody else.

The message travels quickly from one cell to the next one, along little highways called neuropathways. There are thousands of these pathways that carry messages to specialized areas of the brain. It's comparable to a network of highways that lead to different regions or cities.

At any point in time several stimuli may be competing for your attention at once. You are able to see, hear, touch, smell, and taste all at the same time. This often means you have to make a concentrated effort to select the important from the unimportant stimuli around you. Right this moment you are attending to the words and ideas on the pages of this book. At the same time, there may be a radio playing in the background, your body is pressing against the chair, the smell of coffee emanates from the kitchen, and children are talking in the other room. Concentration requires that all of these background stimuli be suppressed so you can make sense out of the ideas in this book. You may even have a light cold, but are still able to focus on your reading.

When you make extra effort to concentrate, your brain releases added neurotransmitters. These additional messengers cause the messages to travel a little more quickly and enable you to focus. You are able to concentrate on one stimulus source and block out the others.

Children and adults with attention deficits do not seem to manufacture extra neurotransmitters. The absence of sufficient dopamine appears to be responsible for this inability to produce sufficient neurotransmitters. As a result, all messages come in at once with equal impact. The person is not able to suppress one and focus on the most important element. The result is like a gridlock on a freeway system when everyone is trying to get to the same place at the same time. The system can't handle it and traffic comes to a halt. Radiators boil over, tempers flare, and apparently random reactions ensue.

The neurophysiological explanation of attention deficit helps us to understand how stimulant medication works. Stimulant medication increases the production or release of neurotransmitters, allowing the person to focus on the most important message being sent.

Now let's look at the *dopamine* connection in a little more detail. Studies of cerebral spinal fluid in ADHD and normal children have shown there is decreased brain dopamine in ADHD children. Some studies show that when ADHD is treated with medication, there is improvement in the metabolic changes of dopamine seen in the spinal fluid. With what has been published so far, the evidence seems to say that ADHD children have a selective deficiency in the availability of dopamine.

Additional support for the dopamine hypothesis comes from the epidemic encephalitis of 1918. This disease produced Parkinsonism in adults and ADHD symptoms in children. Research has shown that Parkinsonism results from dysfunction of the dopamine system. This close association between ADHD and Parkinsonism suggests a common cause may be in the dysfunction of the dopamine pathways.

Animal studies have also shown increased activity and difficulty with certain kinds of learning are not produced by damage to a specific location of the brain. Rather, the ADHD-like symptoms are a result of damage to the nerve-cell endings that deliver dopamine throughout the entire brain. When the dopamine-containing nerve endings in rats were destroyed, they could not utilize the dopamine system throughout the brain. The resulting symptoms were just like ADHD in humans. Further, when the rats were given methlphenidate (Ritalin®), their behavior improved.

From this research it appears that children with attention

deficit are born with a shortage of neurotransmitters or a dopamine deficiency. The frontal lobe of the brain is the area most responsible for controlling attention, activity, and the ability to plan ahead. It is assumed there is a connection between ADHD and the shortage of neurotransmitters that affects primarily the frontal lobe.

Attention Center Model

Several researchers have proposed a brain-based model of ADHD to try to bring all the above information together. We start with the idea of an *attention center* within the brain that utilizes dopamine. This center has input from other areas of the brain, such as the frontal lobe. After this attention center gets a message, it communicates with the rest of the brain to regulate the degree of attention and concentration. If the child is trying to understand a concept in the classroom, the center could be set for intense concentration. Or, this center could be set to allow the child to be easily distracted, as would be appropriate on the playground. Perhaps we could think of a hearing aid as an example. I recall a man in our church who frequently had to adjust his hearing aid. If he was engaged in a conversation with you one-on-one, he would turn up his volume so he could catch all of what you had to say. But if he was in a group of people, say in the fellowship time after a service, he would turn down his hearing aid so that the background noise and multiple conversations didn't overload his system.

This same idea might apply to our attention center. When we need to focus, the system turns up the concentration level through a biochemical reaction. When we need to be more aware of everything around us, the system turns down the concentration level. Children who have ADHD are unable to utilize the normal brain-stem attention center to adjust levels of attention and concentration in the manner available to normal children.[10]

In summary, the current theory about ADHD is that there is a genetic tendency toward dopamine depletion in a specific part of the brain. This frontal lobe area is responsible for planning and attention, as well as for inhibiting overreactivity.

Research suggests that chemical pathways utilize dopamine neurons to manage the needed levels of attention. ADHD occurs because of a system dysfunction which causes a type of barrier. This barrier results in behavioral disinhibition and diminished sensitivity to behavioral consequences or rules.

Children without this genetic predisposition can develop ADHD through illness or injury, but this rarely happens. At this time, there is very little evidence that ADHD can arise purely out of social or environmental factors, such as family dysfunction, diet, toxins, or faulty parenting.

Questions about Causes of ADHD

1. Does vitamin deficiency seem to play any part in children with attention deficit?

Vitamins are nutrients essential to growth and development and to practically every aspect of body function, including the brain and its function. The body does not manufacture vitamins, so they must be taken in with food. It makes sense that we would wonder about some kind of vitamin deficiency which could affect a person's ability to attend. The two approaches to investigation are, first, look at ADHD children to see if their body chemistry shows any significant pattern of deficiency, and second, to administer various doses of vitamins and observe for improvement in behavior. So far, there are no conclusive studies.

Some health food devotees and nutritionists have advocated massive ingestion of certain vitamins for the treatment of ADHD, assuming some type of deficiency is the cause of attention problems. However, carefully controlled studies have failed to show that megavitamins are effective in reducing the symptoms of ADHD children. Of additional concern is the risk of blood levels reaching toxic levels from too many vitamins. Too much of anything can be dangerous.

Regular multivitamin supplements generally do no harm, and might help cognitive function. Megavitamin therapy can cause liver damage or interfere with normal vitamin metabolism. Since there is no clear evidence of benefit, the treatment has nothing to recommend it in addressing any causes of ADHD.

2. Does fluorescent lighting contribute to problems with attention and distractibility?

In the mid-1970s it was proposed that cool-white fluorescent lighting emitted certain soft X rays and radio frequencies that could cause children to become hyperactive. Since many schools use such lighting in classrooms, it was argued that this lighting increased the activity of children in these classrooms, and could even make some clinically hyperactive.

The initial study was very poorly designed and methodologically flawed. Subsequent studies corrected the problems and no effects of lighting condition were found. This idea appears to have no support.[11]

3. A lot of adopted children seem to have ADHD. What is the relationship?

Research suggests the rate of ADHD in adopted children is four times higher than among nonadopted children. This means about 20 percent of all adopted children have the symptoms of attention disorder. The incidence is only about 5 percent for birth children. No one knows why this is true.[12]

Our current understanding is that ADHD evolves from a conspiracy of factors which interact to form an impulsive child. We are sure there is not a simple explanation that would apply to the bulk of children considered hyperactive. This applies to all children, both birth and "chosen."

References

1. Anderson, P., "Schools Brace for 'Crack Kids,' " *The Seattle Times/Seattle Post-Intelligencer* 4 August 1991:A2.

2. Ferguson, H.B., and Rapoport, J.L., "Nosological Issues and Biological Variation," *Developmental Neuropsychiatry,* ed. Rutter, M. (New York: Guilford Press, 1983), 369–84.

3. Nelson, K.B., and Ellenburg, J.H., "Apgar Scores and Long-Term Neurological Handicap," *Annals of Neurology* 6.1982 (1979): (Abstract).

4. Barkley, R.A., *Attention-Deficit Hyperactivity Disorder. A Handbook for Diagnosis and Treatment* (New York: The Guil-

ford Press, 1990).

5. Taylor, E.A., "Childhood Hyperactivity," *British Journal of Psychiatry* 149 (1986):562–73.

6. Conners, C.K., *Food Additives and Hyperactive Children* (New York: Plenum, 1980).

7. Kaplan, B.J., et al., "Dietary Replacement in Preschool-Aged Hyperactive Boys," *Pediatrics* 83 (1989):7–17.

8. Hagerman, R.J., and Falkenstein, A.R., "An Association Between Recurrent Otitis Media in Infancy and Later Hyperactivity," *Clinical Pediatrics* 5 (1987):253–57.

9. Conners, C.K., *Feeding the Brain: How Foods Affect Children* (New York: Plenum Press, 1989).

10. Goldstein, S., and Goldstein, M., *Managing Attention Disorders in Children* (New York: John Wiley & Sons, 1990).

11. O'Leary, K.D., Rosenbaum, A., and Hughes, P.C., "Fluorescent Lighting: A Purported Source of Hyperactive Behavior," *Journal of Abnormal Child Psychology* 6 (1978):285–89.

12. Maxey, D.W., *How to Own and Operate an Attention-Deficit Kid* (Charlottesville, Virginia: HAAD, 106 South St., Suite 207, Charlottesville, VA 22901, 1989).

13. Zametkin, A.J., et al., "Cerebral Glucose Metabolism in Adults with Hyperactivity of Childhood Onset," *New England Journal of Medicine* 323 (1990):1361–66.

ChAPTER ThREE

HOW DO I FIND HELP?
The Assessment of ADHD

Honey, have you finished that book about attention disorders?" Julie asked her husband, Jeff, after the kids had left the dinner table.

"Yes," he responded. "I thought it pretty much hit the nail on the head as far as describing things with Danny."

"That's what I thought." Julie sighed. "I couldn't believe it when the author started describing how kids with attention deficit act. It was like every page was a day out of Danny's life. I cried the whole time I was reading it."

"Yeah, it hit me kind of hard too. I guess the next question is what we do now," Jeff pondered. "I know his teacher has been telling us something is wrong. In fact, didn't she give us that book?"

"She did," Julie answered, becoming a bit more agitated. "Remember, we have a conference with her next week. Maybe she will give us some ideas about how to get help. I know I need it. If something isn't done to calm him down, I'm going to run away and live in a mountain shack in the Siskiyous!"

ADHD is a real and dramatic part of the lives of many families. I assume such conversations have taken place around thousands of dinner tables. Countless concerned and frustrated parents have struggled with the question of where to turn for help.

After reading the earlier chapters, you may believe your child has attention deficit and/or hyperactivity. Maybe a teacher or friend has suggested that your child might have ADHD. Whatever the reasons for your suspicions, you are now wondering where to turn for help. In this chapter, I will discuss what to expect from the assessment and treatment process and how to find the right professional.

Expectations of Treatment

Before you proceed to look for a care-provider, you need to consider what you expect out of treatment. Then you can select an approach that will be most appropriate for your goals.

● *ADHD is managed, not cured.* Treating ADHD will not make it go away. Your child's inattention, overarousal, distractibility, and difficulty in keeping rules are inborn behavioral and temperamental characteristics. They are part of his very nature. These qualities will stay with him throughout his life to one degree or another. Treatment can improve a child's chances for avoiding many of the long-term problems associated with ADHD. There is every reason to believe your son or daughter can have a very productive life. At the same time, you need to remember this objective will require long-term help. Both you and your child will need to commit to the continuous effort of managing the situation in the best possible manner.

● *Treatment of ADHD does not consist only in correcting a problem within your child.* The child is not the only one who has to change in the process of dealing with ADHD, although he is certainly the focal point. Self-management and self-control are crucial objectives for your child. However, family members and teachers must also be willing to look at how their actions impact the child's difficulties with impulsivity and inattention. Managing the ADHD child involves both modifying his behaviors and altering his environment to obtain a better fit.

For example, a student may have difficulty attending to instructions and turning in assignments. Treatment must focus on the child's inattention. But at the same time, the child's teachers will need to find ways of encouraging the child, providing structure, and pacing requirements to his abilities. Parents must learn to use positive rather than negative reinforcement. The family climate will need to be altered from constant tension and frustration to clear structure, but with reason and tolerance. This may require an adjustment in your expectations so that your child can meet them. Parents need tools for dealing with conflict and problem-solving, as well as help in self-care and avoidance of burnout. In short, the entire system for the ADHD child will need some adjustments.

• *Each ADHD child requires a different plan.* Children with ADHD are more different than they are alike, even though we use a common term like attention deficit or hyperactivity. Your child has unique strengths and weaknesses that must be considered when designing a program that will help him achieve his full potential. Treatment must also be customized to the needs of your family. A family with only one child has a much different dynamic than one with four children. A diagnosis of ADHD for a family in financial crisis will demand a greater support system than for a family that has financial security.

• *Treatment must be multidimensional.* Usually treatment will need to be multifaceted. For example, medication may be used to help control some of the child's inattention and overarousal. Yet medication does not give the child the skills to organize note cards for a term paper, or to make friends. These skills must be addressed by a coordinated effort of teachers, mental health professionals, and family.

A multidimensional approach to treatment is also suggested by the limited long-term effects of medication alone. Medication can have modest long-term beneficial effects on overactivity and impulsivity, but very little on the social and academic aspects. Research has shown that children who receive multimodal treatment have a better long-term outcome than do children who are treated with medication alone.[1]

Multidimensional treatment has another advantage over medication alone. It allows the child to have more of a sense of ownership and control by being less dependent on medication. It can reinforce a feeling of mastery in the child. An example would be the feelings of accomplishment in a child who has worked hard on his social skills. When friends finally start to invite him to spend the night, he knows it is a result of behavioral changes he has made in himself, and not the medication alone. A treatment effort that draws on all aspects of the person builds on this sense of personal accomplishment and self-esteem. It truly is skills as well as pills.

• *An evaluation should be comprehensive.* One reason an evaluation is so important is that you need to determine accurately *why* your child is having trouble with inattentiveness, impulsiveness, and overarousal. Treatment will vary depending on the underlying problem. Other problems can masquerade as ADHD. For example, an anxious, worried, or even depressed child can be inattentive and fidgety in the classroom. An abused child can be very distractible and disorganized. Students with learning disabilities can appear inattentive when their underlying problem is difficulty with language processing. Treatment for each of these problem areas is quite different, making a comprehensive evaluation very necessary.

A proper diagnosis orients the child, parents, and other care-givers to the general nature of the child's difficulties. In doing so, it provides information about a child's strengths and weaknesses. Assessment procedures help identify which situations are particularly troublesome for a child and which situations are more comfortable. The assessment should also identify the child's particular academic strengths and weaknesses so that the educational program can achieve maximal results.

A complete and thorough evaluation is important for another reason. The severity of ADHD itself is not the crucial predictor of long-term adjustment. Coexisting problems such as learning disabilities, conduct disorder, poor peer relationships, and disruptive family relationships play a key role in determining future health. A comprehensive assessment is needed to determine if some of these additional factors are present, along with the ADHD. Treatment will then be needed, as appropriate, for each problem area.

Where to Find Help

There are several considerations in selecting an appropriate professional to coordinate your child's care. First, you want that person to be competent in assessing and treating ADHD. This person should also be experienced in working with children, and should have up-to-date knowledge about attention deficit.

Second, you want to know if the professional is able to oversee a multidimensional approach to treatment. A key ingredient in this approach is a close tie with the child's school. Teachers are a crucial source of information about many of the areas associated with attention deficits. A teacher can report on how the student attends in class, relates to peers, responds to structure, handles transition periods, and acquires academic skills. Information from the teacher is needed for both diagnosis and treatment. Yet some clinicians initiate very little contact with the school. Many times as I am talking with a child's teacher or other school personnel, they will tell me how unusual it is to hear directly from the child's primary therapist. If the professional you choose does not invite close communication with the school, your child will not be well served.

Most clinicians have a general theoretical orientation to the management of mental health problems, and a competent mental health professional or physician will fit the treatment to the problem. However, some professionals have a rather fixed approach to managing nearly all mental health problems. Some will deal with childhood problems as manifestations of family disturbances. They tend to work with the entire family right from the beginning and spend no time evaluating the child.

Other professionals see symptoms of ADHD as mostly a

by-product of inner psychological conflicts and sexual or aggressive impulses. Their focus is aimed at resolving internal conflict through self-awareness. Finally, some professionals take a strictly medical or neurological approach to ADHD and minimize the importance of school-based intervention.

Each of these approaches can be a legitimate way to deal with some mental health problems. They can even be a part of the total effort for ADHD children and their families. The important point is for the professional to have sufficient perspective to include all aspects of diagnosis and treatment in the management plan.

ADHD is a complex disorder which works its way into all levels of a child's life. It represents more than any one of the orientations mentioned earlier. Therefore, *the most helpful professional is one who will gather information from multiple sources and arrive at a diagnostic decision based on a reasonable integration of the data.* For a problem this chronic and multifaceted, you need someone who is willing to get involved with the diversity of issues that arise at home, in school, and within the community.[2] This person may be a psychologist, psychiatrist, pediatrician, neurologist, or child therapist. The critical factors in your selection are a willingness to work with community agencies such as the school, and specific training and experience in the area of ADHD.

As the primary advocate for your child, you must take the initiative to secure the best help available. Ask questions, become informed, and read everything you can get your hands on. This allows you to challenge and ask about those things that don't make sense to you. Your goal here is to be an active collaborator in the process. When you call or meet with a professional, ask if he or she has had specific training in the diagnosis and treatment of ADHD. What kind of professional workshops has s/he attended? How many children has s/he evaluated? How involved does the professional become in the monitoring of treatment? If you or your child has a problem, how available is the doctor to respond?

You need to feel comfortable and confident with the practitioner. If s/he won't answer your questions or gives unclear answers, look elsewhere. When you are uncomfortable with a practitioner's personality or professional approach, confront the issue or find someone else. This is too important an issue to tolerate incompetency or unprofessional conduct.

At the same time, let me remind you there are no immediate cures or quick answers to the problem of ADHD. If you go looking for a doctor to immediately eliminate all stress and strain from your life, you will always be disappointed. Likewise, if a professional promises you quick fixes, charges unusual fees, and offers unorthodox methods, you should get out of there right away.

The following checklist summarizes our discussion. Use it as you review your contact with various professionals.

Checklist for Selecting ADHD Professional

☐ Has appropriate professional degree and licensing—Ph.D., Psy.D., Ed.D., M.D., M.S., M.S.W., etc.

☐ Has experience working with ADHD children.

☐ Has specific training in assessment and treatment of ADHD.

☐ Is able to manage a multidisciplinary or multimodal approach to assessment and treatment.

☐ Is able and willing to work closely with your child's school and teacher.

☐ Seems to appreciate complex nature of ADHD and is able to draw on many community resources to help your child.

☐ Has balanced perspective on ADHD. Recognizes the long-term nature of the problem, but is encouraging about degree of help available.

☐ Makes no promises of instant cures or proposes unorthodox procedures.

☐ Was recommended by satisfied client or some other professional familiar with their work.

☐ Has a sensitivity and ability to deal with spiritual issues. Is a Christian who can relate faith and practice to your needs.

● *How to find help.* With these characteristics and objectives in mind, you are now ready to set out to find a coordinating professional. Many referrals of this type are made through former clients. Talk to other parents who may have had similar problems with their children. See if they have any recommendations. Parent support groups often keep track of qualified and responsive clinicians. In Part Three I have included national offices for several such groups that can direct you to local or state chapters. Your child's teacher or school personnel may be able to give you a list of respected professionals in your area.

Sometimes there is a well-regarded specialty clinic or individual practitioner in your area with a reputation for working with ADHD. Look up Christian counseling centers and ask if they have a person on staff who specializes in this. Your pastor could also be a source of information for Christian professionals and counseling centers. Your family doctor or pediatrician can probably refer you to outside help, as well as be a place for you to begin your inquiry.

If your area has a medical center or university, you might call the child psychology or psychiatry departments and ask where such services can be obtained. Some cities have medical and mental health referral bureaus that list various practitioners and specialties. You can call or write these agencies and get several names.

You may live in an area where there isn't anyone with specific expertise in handling referrals for ADHD. In that case you might have to travel to the closest available specialist. Most large cities will have someone who can provide the help you need. Write or call the person or agency and arrange to go in for an evaluation. Some of the preliminary work can be done by mail. Forms can be sent to you to complete and distribute to teachers; these are then returned prior to your initial visit. The interviews, family history, and testing can often be completed in one or two days, if a concentrated schedule is needed. Make sure you have exhausted your local resources before traveling outside your area. It's best if there is a professional close by who can easily be consulted and who is familiar with the local resources and schools. An opinion 200 miles away is no more accurate than competent help from someone close at hand.

Your first choice might be your family physician or pediatrician. If so, you can ask your doctor about his willingness and competency to coordinate the efforts for your child. He may refer you to someone more knowledgeable or recommend an outside consultation. Some developmental pediatricians are very conversant with ADHD and have a treatment plan they utilize. Many physicians, while they can prescribe medication, may not be familiar with the schools and specifics of educational and personal intervention techniques. In that case, they would need an additional resource such as a psychologist or child therapist.

Sometimes a physician will refer patients with suspected ADHD to a child neurologist. A neurologist can rule out other possible medical problems, but usually does not have access to the behavioral and educational strategies. However, neurologists are useful when there is suspicion of seizures, brain damage, or Tourette's syndrome. For most ADHD children, extensive neurological tests such as an EEG, CAT, and PET scans are not necessary. Seldom do they turn up anything, unless there are strong or suspicious neurological or medical symptoms.

Child psychologists are often the professionals most familiar with ADHD. They are usually the most comfortable with behavioral, educational, and social approaches to treatment. Psychologists cannot prescribe medicine and would need to work with the physician to get the medical assessment. A psychologist can usually provide the necessary forms to help evaluate the outcomes of the various types of intervention, including the medication trials.

Child psychiatrists have the medical degree that allows them to prescribe medication. They should have the orientation toward management of ADHD and working with other professionals.

Both a psychologist and a psychiatrist would be able to work with the child and the family on issues of stress, anger management, depression, and conflict resolution.

• *Resources through your local school district.* Before looking elsewhere, you should be aware of free evaluations through your local school district. Intelligence, achievement, speech, language, and motor development evaluations are available under Public Law 94-142. ADHD has only recently become more clearly eligible for special services.[3] The school has an obligation to meet your child's needs to the extent its resources allow. Even if your child is in a private school or is being home-schooled, an educational needs assessment should be available through the public school. Since you pay taxes, you are entitled to receive these services. I have described the process for obtaining services in chapter 7. You might want to jump ahead and look at the first part of that chapter.

Since the school needs to be part of the total planning for your child, it is a very good idea to get them involved as early as possible. Whether or not you utilize the resources of your local school district at the beginning, your child's teacher will still be a vital part of the treatment plan. As I have said, part of choosing an outside professional is selecting someone who is skilled and able to work closely with the school. The communication loop must include the teacher. You can start with the school and eventually involve medical and mental health professionals from outside the school. If you start with an outside professional, he or she will subsequently need to work with the classroom teacher. It doesn't matter so much where you begin the process; just make sure all the necessary resources are included.

A major reason for starting the process within your local school is the issue of cost. However, you might want a second opinion or might not want to wait the ninety days or more that the process often takes in the schools. Perhaps you desire a Christian evaluator involved in the process. You are always free to do whatever you think is best for your child. I just want you to know your options.

Assessment Procedures for ADHD

Regardless of who directs the process, a proper diagnosis of ADHD must include observations and data representing all aspects of a child's life. The coordinating clinician will obtain detailed information from the parents. This will include both current descriptions of the problem and developmental information about the child and family. The clinician will also need objective observations provided by the child's teacher(s) and a physician's medical evaluation. Finally, there will be a clinical interview of the child, and the completion of formal diagnostic testing. I will describe each of these components so you have an idea of what to expect. Then we will look at how it is all put together for confirming a diagnosis of ADHD.

● *Parent information.* The assessment process usually begins with an intake interview with one or both parents of the child in which the clinician asks you to give an overview of the child's problem. This will lead to a discussion of your own history to determine if you experienced similar problems when you were young. Many other aspects of the child's developmental history, disciplinary methods, and prior professional contact will be covered.

You may receive various questionnaires and rating scales prior to your first session with the clinician. If completed prior to the first interview, these can save time and increase the accuracy of recall during your appointment. Together, the detailed interview and the history form should give the counselor an accurate picture of the child's developmental patterns.

Observation of your interaction with your child is important. The counselor may have you spend some time together in a playroom setting or interview all of you together. Sometimes the clinician may even want to make a home and/or school visit.

The parent interviews and background information forms need to be accompanied by objective parent report questionnaires. I will give a brief summary of the most common forms. Not all clinicians use the same instruments. But this listing will give you a fairly accurate summary of the procedures used by the respected authorities in the field. The most widely used and best researched forms are the *Conners Parent Rating Scale* and the *Child Behavior Checklist.*

The *Conners Parent Rating Scale* has been revised to forty-eight items. Each item is scored on a four-point scale which includes: Not at all, Just a little, Pretty much, and Very much. Ten of those items are used to compute the hyperkinesis index which include descriptors of excitability, impulsivity, excessive crying, restlessness, failing to finish things, distractibility, inattention, being frustrated in efforts, disturbing other children, and wide or drastic mood changes.

The *Child Behavior Checklist—Parent Form (CBC)* was developed by Achenbach to record behavioral problems and competencies of children ages two through sixteen. In the *CBC,* the parent or caretaker rates behavioral descriptions as: Not true, as far as you know, Somewhat or sometimes true, or Very true or often true.

The CBC also contains questions concerning the child's social activities and social interaction. Information from these items is used to calculate age and sex-referenced social competence scales.

To assess the impact of the child's possible attention disorder upon home and community situations, the *Home Situation Questionnaire—Revised (HSQ-R)* is often used. You are asked if your child has problems paying attention or concentrating in a number of home situations such as playing alone, getting dressed, at the store, in the car, and when asked to do homework. If you indicate a problem, then you are asked to rate how severe the problem is on a scale of one to nine. The HSQ-R yields scores for the number of problem settings and the average severity of the problem.

For adolescents, clinicians sometimes use an *Issues Checklist for Parents and Teenagers.* The *Issues Checklist (IC)* assesses self-reports of specific disputes between parents and teenagers. It consists of issues that can lead to disagreements between parents and their teenage children, such as chores, friends, and homework.

The *Conflict Behavior Questionnaire (CBQ),* is another self-report inventory that can be used to assess perceived communication and conflict between parents and adolescents. The separate versions for each parent and teen contain true-false items that reflect general arguments, misunderstandings, the inability to resolve disputes, and specific verbal and nonverbal deficits.

The information from the *IC* and *CBQ* can be helpful in tailoring a family therapy program, particularly in the areas of communication skills, problem-solving, and conflict resolution. Repeated administration can monitor progress and assess change.

• *Teacher reports and school functioning.* A careful and detailed school history is essential to obtain a clear diagnosis of ADHD. The clinician will need to understand any progression or continuance of concentration and attention problems. Earlier report cards, teacher comments, and periodic achievement tests, along with previous testing reports, need to be reviewed. If you have copies of these items, take them along for the counselor to evaluate. It will save time if you make copies to leave with the counselor. It also insures that your originals won't be lost.

Descriptions from various school situations and teachers are also needed. Most ADHD children do not have equal behavioral difficulties in all school situations. If we can get a picture of where the child is more successful, it gives us an initial understanding of his coping skills. This data not only helps confirm the ADHD diagnosis, but also gives the counselor ideas for setting up a treatment plan.

The *Conners Teacher Rating Scale* has become a widely used and researched questionnaire for teacher rating of attention disorder behaviors. The revised form contains items that yield three factors: conduct problems, hyperactivity, and inattentive-passive. The scale also is scored for a ten-item hyperkinesis index. The format is identical to the Parent version described earlier.

Another instrument that has been developed in response to statistical and definitional criticisms of the Conners Scale is the *ADD-H Comprehensive Teacher Rating Scale (ACTeRS)*. The teacher completes each description of the child on a five-point scale. Sample items include: works well independently, follows simple directions accurately, overreacts, and acts or talks without thinking. This scale is also reported to be quite sensitive to medication influences, and might be used to monitor your child's behavior during medication trials.

The *Child Behavior Checklist—Teacher Report Form (CBC-*

TRF) by Achenbach is a parallel form to the Parent version described earlier. It contains much of the same information as the Parent form. Different scales have been developed to reflect the child's work habits, level of academic performance, degree of teacher familiarity with the child, and general happiness of the child.

The *School Situations Questionnaire—Revised (SSQ-R)* is the equivalent version to the *Home Situations Questionnaire.* The teacher responds to eight school situations, indicating whether or not a student has problems paying attention or concentrating. If yes, the teacher indicates the severity. The useful scores are the number of problems settings and the average severity.

A final rating scale that can be completed by the classroom teacher is the *Academic Performance Rating Scale.* This scale assesses a child's productivity and accuracy in completing schoolwork. While this information can be inferred from report cards, this form also contains questions that deal with attention and organization skills. This can shed more light on the child's attention deficits, as well as provide more clues about how the child approaches his work. This will be very useful in implementing practical suggestions during the intervention phase of the procedures.

Clinicians need to remember that teachers are busy people and have twenty to forty other children to manage. Most of the forms mentioned here take only a few minutes to complete. I usually have parents deliver the forms to their child's teacher with instructions and a return envelope with my address. That way the teacher is able to send the forms directly to me. Sometimes teachers will be a bit more candid in their comments if they know the parents are not receiving the forms.

Clinical Assessment of the ADHD Child

A few months ago my car wouldn't start right away. We had to crank and crank to get it running. Several times my wife sat in the church parking lot fussing with the car before it would start. I took it to the shop and guess what happened. You're right—it started perfectly. They even kept it for a couple days and the crazy thing started right up each time. They sent me home with a bill but no diagnosis.

You get my point. To the utter bewilderment of mothers, highly active, destructive, and inattentive children have come to my office and acted like angels. Even if they have just been picked up at school for fighting in the lunch room and setting off the fire alarm, they are able to smile and make pleasant conversation.

If I didn't know better I might look at such a child, have him play a few minutes of video games on my computer, and conclude he was a pretty normal kid. On the other hand, I might look at Mom and see her eyes bugging out and veins popping from her neck. My conclusion could be the child doesn't need medication, but Mom does.

The error here is to jump to a conclusion from nonrepresentative data. An accurate diagnosis of ADHD must be made from a variety of sources, in different situations, and across several samples of time. That is why we need to collect the many different observations from alternate sources in order to get a clear picture of how the child really acts. (By the way, my car still has trouble starting at random times, and no diagnosis has yet been made.)

● *Clinical measures of attention disorder.* Structured psychometric testing has the potential to provide the clinician with standardized, norm-referenced data about the child. Both quantitative and qualitative data can result from testing designed and administered well. However, in spite of the extensive research on ADHD, there is still no single test or battery of tests that have been shown to be *the* test for diagnosis of attention disorders. The most common psychometric tests used for the attention-deficit child include tasks that measure *reflection, vigilance,* and *sustained attention.* None of these tests are pure measures of attentional ability and questions are frequently raised about reliability and validity. But with caution and understanding, the competent evaluator can utilize some of these tests to obtain *quantitative* objective data regarding the child's attention-related skills. Also, important *qualitative* observations can be made about the process the child goes through while responding to the test items.

Several clinic-based tests of sustained attention and impulsivity have recently been standardized for use in evaluating symptoms of ADHD. Some of the most widely studied laboratory measures of vigilance or attention span with the ADHD population are the *Continuous Performance Tests (CPT)*.

One *CPT* that has been developed recently is the *Gordon Diagnostic System (GDS)*. This is a portable, solid-state, childproof computerized device that administers a nine-minute vigilance task, where the child must press a button each time a specified, randomly presented numerical sequence occurs. The validity and reliability studies are good; this system is able to discriminate ADHD from normal children, and is sensitive to stimulant medication.[4]

The *GDS* is rather expensive, and probably only clinicians who do a lot of ADHD evaluation will be able to justify its purchase. In spite of its expense, the *GDS* is one of the few measures of attention that has enough available evidence on its psychometric properties and sufficient normative data to be adopted for clinical practice.[5] Like rating scales, the *GDS* provides one source of information to be integrated with the balance of data gathered by the evaluator. You can ask a prospective clinician if they have the *Gordon Diagnostic System,* or something like it. Most probably will not have it. This does not mean their evaluation is inadequate. Remember, there is no single test for ADHD. The *GDS* is, however, a diagnostic tool with a lot of promise.

Other tests are used to measure a child's impulsivity and ability to attend. The *Stroop Word-Color Association Test, Matching Familiar Figures Test,* and the *Hand Movements Test* are some examples. Different clinicians may choose to use various tests, depending on their experience and preferences.

The *Wechsler Intelligence Test for Children (WISC)* is the most common individually administered test for determining a child's general level of academic potential of IQ. The test has recently been revised and is now called *WISC-III.* The test is divided into two sections called Verbal and Performance. Within each section there are five or six subtests which measure different aspects of intelligence and problem solving. Three subtests from the *WISC* have been factor-analyzed into a category called "Freedom from Distractibility." The subtests used are Arithmetic, Coding, and Digit Span. Data is conflicting on whether these subtests can discriminate ADHD children from normal children. Since the *WISC* is often used in determining at least general intelligence, the data from these subtests will frequently be available. Your evaluator may or may not highlight these scores as part of the diagnosis.

• *Direct observation.* Systematic formal behavioral observations in natural settings can be another useful component in the diagnosis and assessment of ADHD children. Direct observations are time-consuming and expensive, and they can also be difficult to standardize. But when combined with parent, child, and teacher interviews and rating scales, observational data can add greater validity, integrity, and rigor to the clinical process.[5]

When possible, I observe the child in the classroom. I may count the number of talk-outs and out-of-seats, compared to on-task behavior. Later I will ask the teacher if that period was a representative sample of the child's behavior. If so, I can compare this with my other classroom experiences. This process does give a better sense of depth to the assessment, and also sets the stage for implementing classroom interventions that are relevant and appropriate. Because I have been there and talked to the teacher directly, I have a better appreciation of what kinds of recommendations to make.

The clinician may give other tests to round out the assessment. The *Piers-Harris Self-Concept Scale* is a brief self-report measure to evaluate self-concept in children and adolescents. Subtitled "The Way I Feel about Myself," the true-false questionnaire is designed to evaluate a child's conscious feelings about himself. This test might be given if a clearer impression of self-esteem was needed.

Many other measures may be used to get at the emotional features of a child. I will often give the *Bender Gestalt*, several types of sentence completion forms, and portions of the *Education Apperception Test, Thematic Apperception Test,* or *Projective Story-Telling Test.* These latter tests show a series of pictures of various types to which the child responds by telling a story about what is happening in that picture. The results give the clinician an idea of the emotional themes a child uses to describe various life situations.

For additional cognitive and achievement assessment, the clinician may give tests such as the *Wide Range Achievement Test—Revised, Peabody Individual Achievement Test,* and all or part of the revised *Woodcock-Johnson Psychoeducational Assessment Battery.* The revised Woodcock-Johnson test is quite comprehensive. Cognitive skills similar to *WISC* results can be obtained, along with reading, math, spelling, and writing achievement levels. This allows the clinician to obtain a clearer definition if learning disabilities are suspected. It also allows us to compare actual achievement levels to the child's potential ability.

Medical Evaluation

It is essential that children being considered for a diagnosis of ADHD have a complete pediatric physical examination. To be useful, however, the exam must be thorough enough to help achieve a diagnosis or identify other accompanying conditions. Your physician's role includes directing the search for a remediable medical cause of ADHD, as well as participating in the multidisciplinary diagnostic evaluation. If and when medication is indicated, your physician will supervise the medication intervention program. To these ends the following *components of a medical evaluation* should be included.[6]

1. The physician tries to determine if there are any medically remediable causes for ADHD symptoms such as hyperthyroidism, pinworms, sleep apnea, iron deficiency, anemia, or medications such as phenobarbital. While not remediable, the interview and examination may explore related disorders arising out of perinatal factors, previous ear infections, brain injury or encephalitis, previous lead poisoning, and heredity. The major purpose here is to provide a differential diagnosis of ADHD from other medical conditions and to treat those problems appropriately.

2. The child's physician will also need to make a decision

concerning the need for medical diagnostic testing. This can range from blood count to an MRI scan. Each test is helpful to exclude specific medical illnesses that can occasionally masquerade as ADHD. Neurological tests such as EEG, CAT scan, and PET scan are not normally needed, but may be useful if the child's neurological history is significant. These tests do not necessarily validate a diagnosis of ADHD, and should not be ordered unless specific indications of other disorders are present.

3. The doctor will conduct an appropriate physical and neurological examination. The research is confusing in regard to the usefulness of soft signs and minor physical anomalies in the diagnosis of ADHD. Revisions in the examination for neurological abnormalities, now called "subtle signs," have been made and offer better discrimination potential.[7, 8] Goldstein and Goldstein recommend assessment of eye movements, finger sequencing, tandem gait, and choreiform movements (a type of finger movement). Storm has recommended the pediatrician conduct a neurodevelopmental exam which includes: minor neuorologic indicators, fine-motor function, language screening, large-muscle skills, temporal/sequential organization, and visual processing.[9]

4. Finally, the physician conducts the baseline evaluation to determine if there are any contraindications to medication intervention, and to serve as a comparison at future reevaluations. Gathering information on risks of possible medication intervention is part of the physician's initial evaluation.

How Is the ADHD Diagnosis Made?

All of the tests have been given, the forms are scored, and now it is time to make sense of everything. How will your clinician go about evaluating the data? The following format has been found useful in analyzing the various sources of information. This approach describes the types of multimodal data necessary to make a diagnosis of ADHD and provides a guide for the integration of the assessment data. In making the diagnosis of ADHD, the following criteria should be considered:[12]

1. *DSM-III-R* diagnostic criteria. This is the most fre-

quently used and best researched definition available at the present time. Therefore the child should meet these criteria. The *DSM-III-R* definition specifies the child should demonstrate at least eight of the criteria. Your clinician may have additional standards for this criteria, depending on the age of your child.

2. Elevated rating scales. The child must score significantly high on at least one questionnaire sensitive to attention problems. Both the parent and teacher ratings should indicate significant concerns for the areas of inattention, overactivity, and distractibility. As described earlier, the most commonly used scales are the *Conners Parent* and *Teacher Questionnaires,* the *Achenbach Child Behavior Checklist,* and the *ACTeRs.*

3. Objective measures. There is no single test that measures ADHD. However, several of the tests mentioned earlier should show deficits in attentional skills such as reflection, vigilance, persistence, auditory memory, impulsivity, and poor visual concentration. The *Gordon Diagnostic System* is an example of an instrument that measures these skills. A number of other tests can also be used.

4. Situational problems. Children with attention disorder will often have difficulties across numerous situations. There should be problems in approximately half of the situations screened on instruments such as the *Home Situations* and *School Situations Questionnaires.*

There is usually a consensus between parents and teachers concerning the severity and frequency of these problems. If there is not agreement between the home and school reports, the clinician will want to carefully consider why there is a disparity. It could result from a difference of opinions from the various raters or from measurement errors. It is also possible that the child is more problem-free in one situation. The more pervasive the behavior, the greater the need for comprehensive intervention.[5]

5. Differential diagnosis. The clinician working with your child must gather sufficient historical, behavioral, and assessment data to rule out or identify the contribution of the following conditions: medical problems, language or learning

deficits, auditory processing disabilities, specific intellectual deficits, and psychological problems of childhood that could contribute to attention disordered symptoms. The most common emotional problems that coexist with ADHD are oppositional defiant disorder and conduct disorder.[10, 6]

6. Attention disorders with and without hyperactivity. It is important to remember the above criteria are probably more true of the attention-disordered child *with* hyperactivity. The child who experiences attention difficulties *without* hyperactivity may not show as many behavioral problems in school or at home. The ADD child without hyperactivity will have difficulties during individual seat work and in small group activities. Otherwise, he may not experience any problems. Overactive and aggressive behavior is easy to see because it disrupts others. The nonhyperactive child may go unnoticed because s/he doesn't make waves and cause trouble. Girls will be the major candidates in this category.

If the above criteria are met, the conclusion can be made that your child has ADHD. The diagnosis may also include other coexisting conditions, and will need to describe whether hyperactivity is present.

The diagnosis should not stop with merely placing a label on the condition. The crucial part of the process is determining the specific treatment plan appropriate for your child.

How an Assessment Becomes a Treatment Plan

At the conclusion of the assessment procedures, you will not leave the doctor's office with a tidy plan drawn out in ten, easy-to-follow steps, but you will have some definite direction to follow. The nature of ADHD requires a continuing effort to manage and deal with its ongoing challenges. The following steps summarize how the diagnostic information described in this chapter is translated into a tentative treatment plan.

1. The major concerns or problem areas for the child are identified and described. This information is gathered through all of the assessment procedures described earlier.

2. The identified problems are clustered or grouped into categories for ease of description. Categories can include: academic, social, emotional, spiritual, and physical. These

broad categories can then be broken down into specific areas. For example, academic can be divided into intelligence and achievement. In turn, these can be divided into their specific components. Achievement, for example, can include reading, math, language, and writing skills. All of the various components of intelligence would also be examined, with any deficiencies or learning disabilities identified for remediation and compensation.

3. The counselor will end up with a broad picture of your child, covering the entire spectrum from academic to medical needs. The diagnosis takes place when these various descriptions of behavior and symptoms are compared to the criteria and guidelines established for all of the disorders of childhood. If your child meets the combined criteria for ADHD as described in chapter 1, then the diagnosis of ADHD would apply, along with any other handicapping conditions.

4. The next step is to prioritize the various problem areas into some type of treatment plan. The list allows you and the clinician to decide which interventions need to be started immediately and which ones can be undertaken later.

5. The clinician will also need to identify the unique aspects of your child's life—what features of your culture, family, marriage, financial condition, community resources, stressors, medical conditions, etc., impact your child. The relevance and practicality of each intervention idea must be evaluated in terms of the context in which you and your child live.

6. Next, a list of the various treatment options is prepared. Intervention ideas are set forth to address the specific needs of your child and family. What kinds of adjustments would help in the classroom? What can parents do at home to help teach self-control and organization? Would medication be appropriate? Dietary changes? Marriage or family counseling? The list goes on until all of the needs are covered.

7. The treatment ideas are then evaluated. What are the pros and cons for your child of each of the proposed forms of intervention? Are the resources present to actually carry out the suggested treatment plan? Are there risks that need to be weighed against possible gains? These kinds of questions

are considered as thoroughly as possible, before the various parts of the treatment plan are implemented.

8. The treatment components are identified and the necessary resources gathered to begin working the plan. As the specific ideas are tried, there is always ongoing evaluation. Is the plan working? What needs to be changed? How can it be done better?

As each part of the plan is implemented, there will be adjustments and changes to fit the conditions. What works for another child may not work for yours. Treatment consists of trying previously established ideas that have been found to help children with ADHD. However, if a given tactic doesn't work, it must be adjusted in some way so that it benefits your child. This ongoing evaluation fits the basic principle in working with ADHD problems, "If at first you don't succeed, try, try again."

Questions about Diagnosis of ADHD

1. Does it matter how old my child is when an evaluation is performed?

Children of all ages can be evaluated for ADHD, although more evaluation options are available for older children. Because they are more verbal, additional formal tests and standardized rating scales are available for children above five or six years of age. For younger children the process will be based more on observation than formal testing.

2. How long does a good evaluation take?

Most assessments can be done in three or four hours. Additional time may be necessary if more details are needed about learning, achievement, or emotional factors. This includes only the time of the coordinating clinician. Medical exams and other special tests would be additional.

3. Do both parents need to be involved?

Absolutely. Input and opinion from both parents are necessary to get an accurate assessment. Intervention must involve both the father and mother, and this will be much more effective if both parents have met with the coordinating clinician. Also, since a complete family history is needed for each parent, it is best if they are both present during the initial interviews. Even if the work schedule of the parents is tight, most practitioners can arrange a time to meet. Just remember, time spent during the assessment may yield future benefits in terms of reduced emotional wear and tear.

In cases where the birth parents are no longer living together, it is still very necessary to see both of them. If too much tension would be created by their coming together, the counselor will arrange to see them separately.

4. Is it okay to take notes or record the feedback session with the clinician?

Most professionals will be glad to let you take notes or tape-record the interview. You will be confronted with a large amount of information, and you may want to hear it again or review your notes. You should also expect a written summary of the assessment. This gives you something concrete to study at your own pace and to give to other professionals and your child's school officials.

It is most important to develop a close collaborative relationship with the professionals involved with your child. If you don't understand the jargon or something doesn't make sense, feel free to ask questions.

5. Wouldn't it be simpler to give a child a trial sample of stimulant medication, and if he improved we would know he was ADHD?

There is a very significant flaw in this "Drug as a Test" strategy. Most children and adults will respond to moderate doses of stimulant medication by becoming more attentive and calm. In other words, children other than ADHD children respond to stimulants in a similar fashion. A positive response to medication is nondiagnostic. It is also true that some ADHD children do not respond to medication. These children would be missed if medication was used as an assessment tool.

6. How can a Christian clinician tell if my child has ADHD, or some type of spiritual problem?

This question probably deserves an entire chapter rather than a few short paragraphs, but I'll do the best I can. There are two general principles to apply here.

The first is the need for spiritual *discernment* by both parents and counselors. To discern is to make a judgment or a distinction. It has one function—to distinguish right from wrong so the right can be promoted and the wrong be eliminated. The question in this context is, "Does this child have a spiritual or psychological problem?" Discernment is not so much a function of the mind as it is a function of the Holy Spirit in concert with our thoughts and experiences.[11]

We are instructed, "If any of you lacks wisdom, he should ask God, who gives generously to all without finding fault, and it will be given to him" (James 1:5). It is instructive to note there are conditions attached to God's promise. Obviously, we must ask. But the request must also be made in faith, without wavering. We must believe and not doubt. The wisdom we request from God will allow us to face those inevitable difficulties with patience and practical insights into life.

The second principle is the dual source of knowledge available to the Christian. Our advantage is that we have access to both God's *natural* and *special revelation.* Natural revelation can be found in the various bodies of knowledge we call psychology, medicine, chemistry, etc. We need discernment, of course, to sort through the truth and fiction within our field of practice. But there is relevant information here because all things were created by God and follow His laws. We can draw upon natural revelation just as an engineer utilizes the laws of physics in designing a car for us to drive to church.

We must be very diligent about seeking God's special revelation as found in Scripture. Without this foundation for comparison and examination, we will certainly become confused, misled, and double-minded. An understanding of God's truth can be used in our evaluation process for ADHD. We just need to be prayerfully cautious that our perspective is not contaminated by various secular assumptions.

By following a thorough assessment process, a Christian clinician will be looking for emotional as well as spiritual sources for the symptoms of inattention and distractibility. This readiness to accept that there is spiritual warfare in this world, and that children can be affected, is a major ingredient in being able to appropriately deal with the problem.

References

1. Bain, L.J., *Attention-Deficit Disorders* (New York: Dell Publishing, 1991).

2. Gordon, M., *ADHD/Hyperactivity: A Consumer's Guide* (DeWitt, New York: GSI Publications, 1991).

3. Moses, S., "Letter on ADD Kids Gets Mixed Reactions," *The APA Monitor* 22.12 (1991):36–37.

4. Gordon, M., "Microprocessor-Based Assessment of Attention Deficit Disorders," *Psychopharmacology Bulletin* 22 (1986):288–90.

5. Barkley, R.A., *Attention-Deficit Hyperactivity Disorder. A Handbook for Diagnosis and Treatment* (New York: The Guilford Press, 1990).

6. Adapted from Goldstein, and Goldstein, *Managing Attention Disorders in Children,* pages 70–71, Copyright 1990, Used by permission of authors and publisher.

7. Denckla, M.B., "Revised Neurological Examination for Subtle Signs," *Psychopharmacology Bulletin* 21 (1985):773–89.

8. Denckla, M.B., et al., "Motor Proficiency in Dyslexic Children with and without Attentional Disorders," *Archives of Neurology* 3 (1985):231–33.

9. Storm, G., "ADHD and the Developmental Pediatrician," *Medications for Attention Disorders and Related Medical Problems,* ed. Copeland, E.D. (Atlanta: SPI Press, 1991), 69–79.

10. Goldstein, S., and Goldstein, M., "The Multi-Disciplinary Evaluation and Treatment of Children with Attention Deficit Disorders," 16th ed. (Salt Lake City: Neurology, Learning

and Behavior Center, 1991).

11. Anderson, N.T., *The Bondage Breaker* (Eugene, Oregon: Harvest House, 1990).

12. Adapted from Goldstein and Goldstein, *The Multi-Disciplinary Evaluation and Treatment of Children with Attention Deficit Disorders,* pages 9, 51–60, Copyright 1991. Used by permission of authors and publisher.

PART TWO

TREATMENT OF ADHD

" 'I will restore you to health and heal your wounds,' declares the Lord."

Jeremiah 30:17

ChAPTER FOur

HOW CAN PARENTS HELP?
Parental Intervention with the ADHD Child

Julie and Jeff sat in their car for a few minutes after leaving Dr. Howard's office. The report on Julie's lap indicated very clearly that Danny had ADHD. The doctor had done a comprehensive evaluation and was very compassionate as she described her conclusions.

As the rain beat down on the roof of their car, Julie thought, *This isn't true ... it is not happening to my child ... my child can't possibly have ADHD ... you must be wrong.*

Jeff gripped the steering wheel until his knuckles were white. His thoughts turned more to anger, *Why didn't Danny's teacher say something last year? What's wrong with these doctors that they don't have some way to cure this thing once and for all? What kind of loving God would allow this to happen to an innocent child? Danny doesn't deserve this.*

"What's going to happen to Danny?" Julie said to no one in particular. "Is he going to be frustrated his whole life? What are we going to do?"

"Do you suppose it's my fault?" Jeff asked. "Dr. Howard said this is probably inherited. I guess it means Danny got this from me. How was I to know? Maybe we shouldn't have had any kids."

"No, honey, it's not your fault. It's not anybody's fault, I guess," Julie responded. "We're both feeling pretty helpless right now. But, as Dr. Howard said, at least now we know what's wrong. We realized Danny wasn't like the other kids Now we know why."

"Yes, I suppose you're right," Jeff said. "It helps to know what the problem is. Now we can begin to help work on the solutions. It's just so frustrating to make sense out of all this."

This dialogue represents the questions and feelings of most parents when they learn their child has ADHD. There is a sense of relief about knowing the exact nature of the problem. Some of the guilt is removed because the parents have learned they didn't cause the problem through faulty discipline. But there is anger, and sadness in hearing that ADHD does not have a cure at the present time, and that the condition is something their child will have to deal with the rest of his life.

Parents need a chance to grieve. If you learn your child has attention deficit, don't be in too big a rush to run out and make all sorts of changes. Take your time. Shed some tears and vent your anger. Punch a few pillows or chop up a cord of wood. Let God know how you feel. Talk to some trusted friends or family members about the situation. Don't try to keep up a false front of confidence and faith when you don't feel strong.

There is "a time to weep and a time to laugh, a time to mourn and a time to dance" (Ecclesiastes 3:4). And yes, there is every reason to have hope. The rest of this book is about how to bring that hope to fruition. But before you can reorient your thinking and behavior to the specifics of dealing with an ADHD child, you need a time to mourn. Allow yourself that expression.

● *Feelings of the ADHD child.* Most children will be confused when they learn about the ADHD diagnosis. They might think there is something terribly wrong with their bodies or brain and even wonder if they are going to die. Some may use this diagnosis as an excuse, saying, "I can't help myself. I have ADHD."

Remember, children go through the same grief process as their parents. They will need time to adjust to the diagnosis and its implications. Your child needs acceptance, love, and understanding. Much as an abused child is told time and time again, so your child needs to hear, *"It's not your fault."*

Most children will be relieved, because now people will realize why he has struggled so much. Adults will now have a greater appreciation for why he has so much trouble paying attention and following the rules. He probably really *wants* to behave, but has had a terrible time doing so.

In the resource section, I have listed a number of books you can use to explain ADHD to your child. Check out one or two of these and read them with your child. *My Brother's a World-Class Pain* is a sibling's guide to ADHD, and might be useful in explaining ADHD to your child's brothers or sisters.

Two videos are also listed. *Why Won't My Child Pay Attention?* is directed to parents. *It's Just Attention Disorder* is designed for children. Both are very useful. More complete descriptions are given in the resource section.

• *How to explain ADHD to your child.* One of your most difficult tasks is to explain ADHD to your child. You don't want to say the wrong thing so that he feels inferior or defective. You also are reluctant to say too little and have him remain uncertain and confused. Some children could take parts of an explanation and use them as an excuse to misbehave. Because of these fears many parents try to avoid the issue, but there will eventually be a day of reckoning. When you do approach the subject, it should be done in ways that are honest and helpful. Ideas drawn from the materials mentioned above can help you compose your explanation. In addition, I want to give you a few pointers.

You do need to explain ADHD to your child. He needs to know that you realize he has a difficult time sitting still, stifling interruptions, and keeping his mind on a job. Without some type of explanation, your child will conclude he is dumb or inferior. He needs to know his academic problems are not his fault. Tell him you understand he is doing the very best he can, but that he has a very real problem which makes it hard for him to concentrate and get his work done. Part of treatment begins with an understanding of the nature of ADHD. Just as I began this book with an explanation and definition, so your child needs the same information at a level he can understand.

You can use the following checklists to help your child identify behaviors that characterize ADHD. The lists itemize some of the things that kids have said about themselves. Read them and have your child make a check mark in the box next to each comment that is just like him or her.

At School...

☐ Teachers are always telling me, "Be quiet. Take your time. Don't rush."
☐ It's hard to keep sitting at my desk.
☐ I often have trouble finishing my assignments or I forget to turn them in.
☐ Sometimes I forget to bring home notes from the teacher or homework assignments.
☐ I often forget what the teacher says when she gives directions or explains things.
☐ Sometimes I get in trouble for talking too much.
☐ Even when I try to listen, I often start daydreaming.

With My Friends...

☐ Sometimes I get angry with my friends.
☐ Other kids don't seem to want to play with me.
☐ Most of my friends are younger than I am.
☐ Adults tell me I am too bossy with other kids.
☐ Kids will often pick on me and tease me.
☐ I wish I had more friends.
☐ Sometimes I crowd into other kids' games.

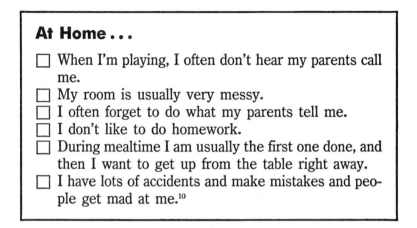

At Home . . .

☐ When I'm playing, I often don't hear my parents call me.

☐ My room is usually very messy.

☐ I often forget to do what my parents tell me.

☐ I don't like to do homework.

☐ During mealtime I am usually the first one done, and then I want to get up from the table right away.

☐ I have lots of accidents and make mistakes and people get mad at me.[10]

The answers to the checklists can now be used to help your child acknowledge that his problems are much like those of many other kids who have attention deficit. You can then go on to give the rest of the explanation.

That explanation needs to be simple and phrased in word pictures your child can relate to. Tell him that every person is unique and that we all have specific strengths and weaknesses. Some people have certain parts of their brain arranged in such a way that they can't see very well. These people wear glasses to allow them to view their world more clearly. Other kids have teeth that need straightening. They wear braces and retainers to correct their teeth so they can eat correctly, play the horn, or whistle.

You might tell a primary-age child something like this: "Danny, your mother and I want you to know what Dr. Howard told us about why it is so hard for you to listen to your teacher and get your schoolwork done. Everybody has little highways in their body, and they have things that work like tiny little cars to carry messages to their brain. If your teacher is telling you how to do a problem, these little "car-like" things called axons have to travel real fast to get all the messages to your brain. Danny, your body doesn't have enough of these little cars or cells. So when the teacher talks to you, all of her ideas don't get to the right place in your brain. In fact, sometimes these little cars run out of gas and never get to the brain at all. But maybe another message *does* get to the brain, like a noise in the room or a bird outside the window. Because these messages don't require you to concentrate so much, it's easier for them to get to the brain; they don't need as many cars. Then what happens is that you pay attention to the broken pencil or bird outside, and miss what the teacher is saying. This isn't your fault. It's just the way your body works."

It's important to let your child know he is not the only one in the world with this problem. There are probably lots of kids in his school who also have attention deficit. If someone else in his extended family has the same problem, share this fact also. There are many parents, even teachers, who have attention problems. Above all, convey your total love and acceptance for your child just the way he is.

Your explanation should be a beginning point for responsibility and problem-solving about how to deal with ADHD. Your comments need to serve as a departure point for discussing how the entire family is going to work together to manage the effects of attention deficit. You want to give a basic definition about the nature of ADHD, and help motivate your child to persevere. Managing the symptoms of ADHD is not easy, but there are many resources to assist you. Let your child know that you, his teacher, and his doctor are going to help.

You can ask your child to describe his problems to you. Various word pictures might emerge: "I have a tiger in my tank." "My engine runs too fast, and I can't make it stop when I want." Or "I'm like the Little Engine That Could, except my engine runs too fast and sometimes jumps off the track." A child who has seen the film *Bambi* would recognize the little rabbit that was rather impulsive and seldom waited long enough to identify the source of a sound.

Each of these descriptions could be turned into a discussion about how to regain control by: "Grabbing hold of the tiger's tail," "Turning off the switch," or "Putting on the brakes." The discussion could then proceed to the specifics of how each of the self-control actions would be accomplished.

Any topic, cartoon character, or metaphor that focuses on channeling energy can be used as a working explanation. It all depends on the child's age and interests and what you can use to hold his attention.[1]

Guidelines for Parenting

ADHD is not so much a skills deficit as a performance deficit. ADHD may not be the result of a lack of cognitive skills, abilities, or strategies. Rather, it may be an inability to apply what the child knows to the demands of a particular setting. ADHD is not a deficit in *knowing* what to do, but in *doing* what you know. This idea helps account for the exasperating tendency of ADHD children to fail to use what they have been previously taught when it is in their best interest to do so.

An ADHD child's problem with motivation regulation may not be successfully addressed by interventions which emphasize skill development. If a major part of a child's problem is a relative insensitivity or "barrier" to social consequences, it means the child is more affected by moment-to-moment events than by general rules or the prospect of future consequences.[3]

Given this view of ADHD, a permanent change in behavior is going to most effectively be brought about by the child's primary caretakers. On a daily basis, it is parents and teachers who must manage the impulsive, disinhibited, inattentive, and poorly regulated behavior for which ADHD children are notorious. You, as a parent, did not cause the attention deficit. Yet, your job is to help your child learn how to manage his own behavior. I will give you five general principles which apply to parenting an ADHD child, followed by some specific strategies to deal with common problem areas.[11]

• The first principle is to *understand the nature of causes for the ADHD child's behavior.* It is important to try to view the world through the eyes of your child and begin to comprehend why he has so much difficulty meeting life's demands. The first three chapters were intended to help you with this component. Other resources are given at the end of each chapter and in Part Three. ADHD parent support groups are another way to extend your awareness about the features of attention deficit.[4, 5, 6]

● A second principle is to distinguish between behavior that results from *incompetence* and that which results from *noncompliance*. You wouldn't punish a four-year-old child because she can't read the newspaper. In the same way, the child's tendency to become overaroused and easily frustrated, as well as impulsive and restless, is unintentional. By successfully distinguishing between incompetent and noncompliant behavior, you can reduce negative feedback and increase compliance and success. This will help stop the development of a more intense oppositional behavior pattern. Your goal is to punish noncompliant behavior and educate incompetent behavior.

Most elementary-age ADHD children cannot be expected to remember multiple directions or commands. If you tell your child to take out the garbage, feed the dog, and go get the mail, you may find garbage in the dog food bowl, and the dog in the mail box. It's simply too much information to process. The result is not noncompliance but incompetence. The child should not be punished for feeding the dog to the mail carrier. This was not an act of willful disobedience. Education is more appropriate. Initially, you need to give one direction at a time. When he can handle it, teach your child to make lists or use memory devices. An example of the latter is to give the child the previous three directions, along with the mnemonic cue of "GDM." This stands for "garbage," "dog," and "mail." The child would then use these prompts to sequence the list of chores.

The question, "Can he help it?" is a tough one. There is no easy way to sort out noncompliance, and you will have many occasions when you probably won't know for sure. You just need to do your best to assess the situation and determine your own course of action. Prayer for God's direction needs to be a daily requirement. Also, pay attention to the angry, defiant, vengeful attitude, as opposed to the accidental, momentary flare-up.

If your child's behavior is aggressive and harmful, I would recommend some type of punishment. The child's reality includes living in a society that censures most forms of violence.

• The third principle is to *teach positive direction.* Most ADHD children hear a lot of "Stop that." "Don't do that." Children who have attention deficit are often raised from an early age with a steady diet of what not to do. These children come to believe that "No!" is the most common word in the world. One parent said her four-year-old daughter was so accustomed to hearing the word "no" following her name that she thought it was part of her name. When some family friends asked the child what her name was, she replied, "Mary No."

It is far more common to point out to a child what is wrong than to give direction on how to do it right. Try not to focus primarily on what is to be stopped. Spend more time demonstrating what is to be started. Attempt to convey to your child ways of *meeting* expectations, rather than punishing him for failure.

One strategy is to tell the child what you want from him, as opposed to what you don't want. Suppose your son has his feet on the coffee table. Tell him, "Please put your feet on the floor," rather than, "Don't put your feet on the table." For the ADHD child to be told, "Don't put your feet on the table," still leaves a whole range of inappropriate things for him to do with his feet. He might put them on the wall, and when his mother complains about that, he could respond, "But I did what you said. I took them off the table."

A better option would be for the mother to say, "Put your feet on the floor under the table." If the child does not comply, it has nothing to do with attention disorder. The behavior is now an example of noncompliance. At this point, negative consequences will prove more beneficial.

• The fourth principle is to consistently expect that *interactions will end successfully.* An ADHD child has a long history of failure. Most often the child has failed to comply to a parent's expectation and is punished. An example might be a daughter who is reprimanded for leaving her toys outside and is sent to her room. It may have been appropriate to use time-out as a consequence for noncompliance. But later, it is essential that the child return to the situation and comply. A primary goal of parenting should be to help your child achieve success. Your daughter needs to eventually pick up her toys. Parents must learn to be very consistent about enforcing this principle. Regardless of how long it takes, the child should eventually comply with your requests. This assumes appropriate and realistic expectations by the parent. Once the child has complied, you then need to provide verbal approval and affirmation for a job well done.[7]

Several good things happen in this sequence. The child learns that compliance is expected through the consistent application by the parents. She was able to practice an appropriate skill. And finally, she was eventually able to receive positive feedback based on success, rather than ending an interaction in failure.

It is also important to measure many aspects of success by effort. Encourage your child to *do* his best, not to *be* the best. Always watch out for the moving carrot. This is the ploy of always making full parental approval just slightly out of reach. Avoid communicating, "Yes, you did a good job, but why didn't you do this other part better?" The child tried his best but gets the message it wasn't good enough. This becomes very discouraging. Offer lots of praise and give rewards generously and frequently. Praise your child for trying, even when he doesn't succeed at achieving the terminal goal. The result will be his continued efforts to try.

• The fifth principle reminds me of the question, "What are the three most important considerations in making a retail business successful?" The answer is, "Location, location, and location." With ADHD children the key considerations are *structure, structure,* and *structure.* A child with attention deficit needs more directions, structure, firmness, structure, consistency, structure, positive reinforcements, and structure than non-ADHD children. This might not be a problem for parents whose style or temperament lends itself to detail and organization. However, other families are more chaotic by nature, the needs of a child are intense, or the temperament of the parent is more casual or informal. To them, the prospect of implementing systematic expectations and follow-through is overwhelming.

Whatever your style, the constant concentration and patience needed for a child with attention disorders can wear down the best parent. There will be days when you are at your wit's end and will seriously consider running away. You've had a terrible, horrible, no good, very bad day, and you feel like giving up, tossing in the towel, and trading in the family station wagon for a one-way ticket to Australia.

The important thing is that even if you have these feelings and thoughts, you won't act on them. You will find a way to process your feelings, and then remember that your loss of control will not help matters. When your child can't control himself, he needs your stability. He will be comforted by your sense of control, but feel frightened and confused when he sees you lose it. This is where God's strength and comfort, along with the support of friends and family, is crucial to your survival. This is also where a general game plan or strategy for behavior management is necessary. The ideas given so far, and the suggestions that follow, will all help establish the structure you and your child need to deal with his impulsive world.

Strategies for Encouraging Compliance

Within the principles outlined above are a number of specific management techniques that need to be taught and practiced. I'll summarize a few of them and give illustrations of each. The purpose of the techniques is to help you react to what your child does in a way that will encourage the repetition of desirable behaviors and discourage unacceptable behaviors.

1. You *pinpoint* the behavior(s) you are concerned about. Think about both *uppers* and *downers. Uppers* are acceptable or desirable behaviors, such as following directions, which you would like to see occur more often. You want their frequency to go up. *Downers* are undesirable behaviors, such as fighting, which you wish to occur less often. You want their frequency to go down.

2. You then *record* the frequency at which these behaviors occur so you know later if things are getting any better. Any simple chart will do the job. Tally marks on the calendar, beans in a jar, or a bar graph will work. Both the A.D.D.

WareHouse and Childswork/Childsplay mail order companies listed in the resource section have charts for this purpose. You usually want to keep track of the count over a constant time period. For example, the number of times a child follows or does not follow directions should be recorded over an entire day, or from the time he gets home from school to bedtime. This record should be kept for the same times from day to day, so the count is comparable.

3. Next you *change* the way in which you are dealing with the behavior, usually using some type of positive or negative consequences. This is the actual *intervention* tactic. You might set up a daily reward if your child has more compliance instances than noncompliance. Every time you give a request, such as "Brush your teeth," or "Feed the dog," a bean goes into the smiley face jar if he complies. If he does not do what you ask in a reasonable fashion, a bean goes into a frowny face or Mr. Yuck jar. At the end of the day, he earns a reward if there are more beans in the smiley jar. I'll give a number of other ideas in the next section.

4. Then you *evaluate* the results of your intervention. The charting system should show whether there is an increase in positive behaviors and a decrease in negative behaviors. Your general impression will usually reflect how things are going. But sometimes behavior changes slowly and you need a daily record to monitor those gradual improvements. I have often worked with parents who bring in the chart, not having paid much attention to it, and then tell me, "Things aren't working. The intervention just isn't doing the job." I say, "Okay, let's look at the chart and see what has been happening." Sometimes I will see that the desirable behavior has improved only modestly over the past two weeks. However, the inappropriate behaviors have dropped by half. The parents haven't been looking at things closely enough. They can't see the forest for the trees. When I point out the gradual improvement, they are more encouraged. This allows them to continue the effort; without the charts, they might prematurely stop a workable idea.

5. The final step is to *try, try again*. If your first form of change didn't work, you redesign the effort and try some-

thing else until it works. If you run out of ideas, your psychologist or other mental health professional can be of help. The ADHD support groups may suggest creative alternatives that have been used by other parents.

● *Examples of the five steps.* To illustrate this process, let me describe an idea I have used for years. The *pinpointed* (step 1) behavior may be leaving personal articles or dirty dishes all over the house. The goal is to get your child (or family) to pick up after themselves. If someone takes a bowl and a glass into the family room to watch TV, you expect the item to be placed in the sink or dishwasher after usage. The same is true for coats, shoes, and toys. When the person is through using the item, it is supposed to be placed in the appropriate storage area—closet, toy box, or storeroom.

For a few days you *count* (step 2) the number of items left lying around the house. This record of items per day left unattended becomes your baseline of comparison.

Next you implement the *change* (step 3) tactic. Through discussion with the child or family members, you suggest the *Sunday Box Strategy.* This is how it works. Whenever an object used by a family member is not returned to its proper storage area, it is placed in the Sunday Box. And the rule is this—any item placed in the box cannot be used until the following Sunday. If the remote control for the TV is left in the laundry room instead of on the TV, it goes into the box and you do without it until Sunday. The same is true for coats, shoes, toys, and maybe even books. You have to use discretion and common sense in regard to schoolbooks and homework. Also, if Dad leaves his billfold or checkbook out on the coffee table overnight, you will have to weigh the value of enforcement versus a ticket for driving without a driver's license.

Each Sunday the box is emptied and a *count* (step 4) is made of all the items, either for the entire family or for each individual. This weekly total serves as the measure of change. The number of items should go down. If it does and then stays down for a few weeks, you can dispense with the box. If people fall into relapse, you can always use it again as needed.

If these ideas don't bring about a desired change, you should look for a way to customize or adjust the initial strategy (step 5). *You try again.* Perhaps you can add a reward, such as a trip to the hamburger stand, if the total one week is lower than the previous week. You keep at it. Try, try again, until the goal is achieved.

Now we will look at additional strategies that can fit into the *change* part of the intervention process. Not all ideas will work equally well with your child. You have to try each one, consistently, using behavior change as the basis of your evaluation. If it works, keep doing it. If not, try something else.

● *Response-cost strategy.* Most parents have used some type of positive reinforcers as a means of motivating their children. Response-cost is a form of punishment and can be a useful tactic. Because many ADHD children do not routinely earn as many reinforcers, or rewards, they can find it difficult to be motivated to earn a reinforcer. Often they will think they can't ever achieve a reward, so they give up trying. The response-cost strategy turns the tables. The child is provided with the entire reward as he goes into a situation and then must work to keep it.

Instead of giving your child a $2 allowance at the end of the week for behaving appropriately, you might place the $2 in nickels in a visible container. As long as your child behaves appropriately the $2 belongs to him. But every time there is an infraction that has been clearly defined and agreed upon between the parents and the child, a nickel is removed from the jar. Because of their unique reinforcement histories, ADHD children perform much better when they are working to *keep* what they already have, rather than to earn something they do not have.[12]

● *Negative reinforcement strategy.* It is important for the parents to be careful about their use of negative reinforcement so that it is employed in a constructive manner. Negative reinforcement occurs when a child works to get rid of an aversive stimulation rather than to earn positive stimulation. Frequently, ADHD children are able to begin tasks, but seldom complete them. This happens in the following way.

A child is supposed to get ready for school. This routine

involves hygiene activities, putting on the proper clothes, collecting needed school supplies, and completing a few chores, such as making the bed. But the ADHD child is distracted very easily and gets off task. Instead of brushing her teeth, the child plays with the hamster. The mother goes into the bedroom, scolds her daughter for dawdling, and insists she brush her teeth. The daughter stops playing with the hamster and heads to the bathroom. Mom sees her moving in the right direction, and so returns to the kitchen to pack the lunches for the day. The mother's scolding is an aversive stimulus. But the scolding stops once the girl starts brushing her teeth. The behavior of starting a new task is reinforced by getting rid of the aversive stimulus, in this case, the mother's negative comments. Mother continues her own work until she sees or hears her daughter preoccupied with another distraction. Again, she reprimands her child, tells her to get her sweater on, but leaves the room when she sees her child begin to get the sweater out of the drawer.

The ADHD child is a victim of a temperament that makes it difficult to persist with a task. But she is also a victim of her learning history that reinforces her for beginning but not completing tasks.

It can be difficult to break this cycle. Here is a way to try to do this. Suppose you send your child off to complete an activity, such as cleaning his room. I would recommend that you repeatedly check on him. This increases the likelihood that when you enter his bedroom he will be engaged in the target task and can be positively reinforced. In the event he is not on task, you then remain with him until the task is completed. The child may work to get rid of the aversive stimulation, in this case the parent staying with him in the room. But he learns that the only way he can do this is to complete the task. The result is a new pattern of task completion, rather than just starting to look busy in order to get Mom or Dad off his back.[12]

• *Cognitive self-monitoring strategy.* ADHD children can function very well if parents identify behavior that results from incompetence and provide external structure and support in response to that incompetence. Cognitive self-monitoring is a technique that provides external clues to assist children in monitoring themselves.

During a play period, instead of coming in and directing your child to speak in an inside voice rather than shouting, you set a timer to ring every ten minutes. The child is instructed that when the timer rings, he is to make certain that his voice level is appropriate and that he is following all the inside playing rules. He then resets the timer and returns to play.

This self-monitoring strategy can also be used to assist a child in morning routines. Together you structure a schedule of required activities and the time allotted to complete the morning routine. Then an audiotape is made by the child in which he directs himself concerning what he is supposed to do at each moment within the sequence of events. He might also include some favorite music on the tape to fill in between the verbal prompts. The music fits the time requirements of each activity in the routine. Each morning the parent comes in and starts the tape, which then acts as an external cognitive cue assisting the child to complete all the necessary morning activities. Over time, the tape can be adjusted with fewer direct prompts, as the child demonstrates his ability to keep to the routine using his own "internal self-talk" to stay on task.[12]

● *Overcorrection strategy.* This is a good intervention for both incompetent and noncompliant behavior. An example would be the child who repeatedly slams the door. Many times the parent might ask the child to return and go through the door in an appropriate manner. When this process is repeated a number of times it is referred to as overcorrection or positive practice.

It is important to approach this situation with a positive attitude and give a very clear message that this is not punishment. If we do not read well, we practice. If we don't kick a soccer ball well, we practice. If we do not close doors well, we also practice. Having the child practice ten times consecutively walking through the door in an appropriate way will increase the chances that the next time he goes through a door, he will do it correctly.

You might also explain that if there is a problem next time, it simply means there was not enough practice, so the number of practice sessions will be doubled. This positive practice routine works with a number of behaviors, such as flushing the toilet, hanging up a coat, or washing hands before dinner.[12]

● *Time-out strategy.* This is a method of removing a child from a problem situation and giving him time to cool off and think about what he has done. Time-out is an appropriate tool for children beween eighteen months and ten years of age. It is most useful for the younger child, and can be instrumental in controlling behaviors such as tantrums, biting, hitting, and throwing things.

Both parents need to agree on the specific behaviors that will result in a time-out. The offenses should be clearly evident, and significant violations of the house rules.

Dullness is the key in selecting the appropriate place for the time-out chair. The child's room is sometimes used for time-out, but a separate quiet spot in a hallway or corner is better. That way his room doesn't become associated with punishment. Besides, there are too many interesting things to do in most children's rooms. A bathroom has the same drawbacks.

The chair should be located where the child cannot see the TV or be within reach of toys. The place should not be dark, frightening, or dangerous. Do not use closets, basements, or attics. This could inadvertently teach your child to be fearful of small or dark places. But the location should be boring. You will also need some type of timer for enforcement.

Before using this technique, explain the entire process to your child. Describe the specific behaviors that will be timed-out. Emphasize that time-out will be used *every time* the child engages in a certain misbehavior. Remember to continue the positive incentive programs to teach appropriate behavior that can replace the misbehavior. Thus, your child can earn stars for playing nicely with his sister, or he can earn time-out for hitting or teasing her. *Never use time-out by itself.* It should always be coupled with techniques that focus on increasing appropriate behavior.

Explain that the time-out begins when he is sitting quietly

on the chair. His bottom must be in contact with the chair at all times. If the child remains on the chair until the timer rings, he can get up and resume activities. If he gets up before the timer rings, you will reset the timer, and the interval starts all over again.

A guideline is one minute of time-out per year of age, up to five minutes. A two-year-old would have two minutes of time-out, a three-year-old, three minutes, and so on. The purpose of time-out is to remove the child from the situation and assure him that you are in control. Five minutes will usually serve that purpose. Longer intervals defeat your purpose. After ten minutes or so, an ADHD child may lose track of why he was timed-out in the first place. Remember though, time-out is to be continuously quiet time.

If your child refuses to comply with the time-out, use a firm, clear voice, and guide him to the chair. If you have to carry him, be firm but not aggressive. Try not to get into physical battles or chase after your child. Retain control and impose additional consequences. Do not use threats. Phrases such as, "Wait till your father gets home," mean nothing to an ADHD child. If your child argues or objects too strenuously, calmly state an additional consequence. Don't use additional time-out beyond a total of ten minutes. You might state that he will see no TV for the rest of the day, or have to go to bed half an hour early.

Warnings have no place in a time-out program. They just teach a child that he has at least one free transgression. Also, don't accept excuses or let the child talk you out of the consequence. Impose the time-out even if your child says, "But Mom, I forgot." Give him five minutes to remember what type of behavior is acceptable. Don't let him throw you off course by saying, "Fine, put me in time-out! I don't care!" This is a form of manipulation. Impose the time-out as planned, and evaluate the effect after a week or two.

Some children may get upset enough to make a mess or create damage while in time-out. If this happens, administer a logical consequence. If he draws on the walls, following time-out he has to clean up the mess. If he breaks the chair, let him know he will have to pay for it out of his allowance, or through extra chores. (The grounding program with various cards could be used here. See the next section.)

When the child's time-out is over, his slate is wiped clean. Don't give a lecture or nag about what happened. You can give a brief reminder about why he went to time-out, along with a simple suggestion for future acceptable behavior. Do not apologize for putting your child into time-out. After all, it was his choice to misbehave. Also, do not require your child to apologize or express regret in order to be able to leave the time-out spot. If he does so spontaneously, be sure to give positive attention. But do not make it a requirement.

Within a few minutes look for an occasion to praise the child for behaving appropriately. If your child went into time-out because of disobedient behavior, such as refusal to pick up his toys or turn off the TV, it is very important to repeat your original command the moment time-out ends. If he refuses to obey, immediately send him back to time-out. If he obeys your request, give him verbal praise. This sequence may need repeating several times (up to ten or fifteen minutes maximum), until the child learns you are serious and consistent about this program. Remember, immediate consequences, whether positive or negative, are important for the child with attention deficit.[2]

If your child misbehaves away from home, calmly point out the misbehavior and inform him there will be a time-out when you get home. Make sure you follow through with the time-out later. Some parents make up "time-out tickets" on small pieces of paper and hand them to the child when he acts out away from home.

Another option is to give time-out on the spot. Find a secluded spot where your child must stay for five minutes. This can be a corner of your friend's house or the back seat of your car. When at the park or some other outdoor setting, you could identify ahead of time a particular tree or bench as the time-out place. This reminds your child the rules still apply, and gives you a definite routine to follow.

• *Grounding strategy.* This method of discipline teaches the child the consequences of improper conduct, while at the same time giving him a chance to earn back privileges through appropriate and responsible behavior. Sometimes we tell a child he is grounded for three days or two weeks. That may seem to work, but the only thing that can end the grounding is that the time runs out.

The form of grounding I am suggesting is a combination of restrictions and work release. It works best in this form with children who are at least eight years old. With adjustments, it can certainly be used with adolescents.

As in time-out, the parents must agree about the rules and infractions. Then they need to sit down with the child and prepare a list of ten jobs that he is capable of doing, but which are not part of his regular assignments. Each job should be roughly comparable in time and effort. Examples might be cleaning the bathroom, raking the front yard, sweeping and cleaning the family room, and so forth.

Each chore is recorded on an index card with a detailed description of all parts of the task. Nothing should be omitted from the listing, so that there is no chance of an argument later about the task criteria. You then explain to the child he will be assigned a certain number of job cards when he breaks an important rule. If he lies about having homework to do, for example, he will pull an assigned number of job cards from the file box, and will be grounded until those chores have been completed.

While grounded, the child must attend school, perform required tasks, and follow house rules. This usually means he must stay in his room unless he is working, eating, or attending school. No entertainment of any type is permitted. Also there will be no contact with friends outside of school and no phone calls. This grounding lasts until every last detail on the job cards is completed. Parents will check to make sure all parts of all chores have been adequately done. If the chores are done correctly, praise your child and end the grounding. If a job requires more work, let your child know exactly what has to be done to end the grounding.[2]

One value of this approach is that your child is actually determining how long he is being grounded. It can take fifteen minutes or two days. The second advantage is that the sequence ends after a positive completion of a task. You are

able to end this chain of events by complimenting your child
for the chores completed.

Additional Strategies for Discipline[13]

● *Size of punishment.* Frequently, partial loss of a privilege is
more effective than a complete loss. Because ADHD children
have a long history of not obtaining positive reinforcement
and of losing many privileges, loss of additional privileges
may have little long-term effect. Restructuring punishment
so that all is not lost as a result of one infraction provides
continued opportunity for the ADHD child to receive at least
partial positive reinforcement.

Let's say your child was ten minutes late coming home for
dinner. You have repeatedly told him not to be late. Rather
than restrict him from going out the whole next day, deduct
an equivalent amount of time, or double the amount of time,
from his free time on the following day. Instead of taking the
child's entire allowance for an infraction, take one-half or
two-thirds. This leaves the child with some money to spend,
but not enough to purchase all that he might want. The mind-
set is what is important here. Rather than have the child
approach the situation knowing that he has nothing and saying he doesn't care, he will have something. It just isn't going
to be as much as he might like.

● *Schedules.* Changes in schedule and routine can be disturbing to any child, but they especially seem to bother ADHD
children. Try to establish consistent schedules within the
home. This includes specific time periods and routines for
morning and evening activities, chores, playtime, television,
and meals. You should also try to explain changes in routine
ahead of time, so that your child can understand and anticipate those changes.

● *Rules.* Clear and concise rules of behavior are essential. I
suggest you work out rules as well as consequences and
write them down. Then post those rules in a prominent place.
Some things might be put in contract form. These expectations should be reasonable, fair, and appropriate to your
child's age. They should apply to other children in the family
as well.

Allow your child choices within the limits of the rules you have set. You want to help develop his initiative and self-control and give a sense of personal influence for his environment.

It is helpful to use charts as a visual reminder of how the rule-governed behavior is going. Consistent management by both parents, from day to day, and from home to school, is also crucial. If a rule is broken and a determination is made that this resulted from noncompliant rather than accidental behavior, negative consequence should follow every time. The same holds true for positive consequences which are to follow appropriate behavior.

● *Instructions.* ADHD children should be provided with simple, clear instructions, frequently accompanied by the use of all three learning modalities—visual, auditory, and physical. This means that you tell your child what you want him to do, and at the same time write it down, draw a picture, use a word picture, or point to some graphic reminder. The physical modality can be used by having the child act out the task, when appropriate. Writing out the assignment also draws on the kinesthetic or physical aspect of learning. Finally, have your child repeat back the instructions and be sure to give him at least verbal reinforcement for understanding and verbalizing the direction. Don't give more than one or two instructions at a time. Earlier I mentioned the use of memory devices. These should be encouraged and practiced. If the task is difficult, break the activity into specific tasks that are smaller, and then sequentially direct your child.

● *Control environmental distraction.* A minimally distracting environment will not guarantee an increase of time spent on a task, but it can help. Use a specific minimally distracted location for homework or other times of concentrated activity. Face the desk toward a blank wall, minimize clutter, and avoid bright distracting colors or patterns in decor. It doesn't work to have the stereo blaring forth while the student is doing homework.

Play should be limited to one or two other children at a time. You also need to take an active role in choosing appropriate playmates so that his most rambunctious friends are not present at the same time. Even when he is playing alone, involve your child in one activity at a time, remove needless background noise such as the radio or TV, and put unused toys out of sight.[7]

● *Natural or logical consequences.* Many times the normal course of events will provide consequences to behavior. If a child goes outside on a cold day without a coat, he may catch a cold. That is a natural consequence. Your child calls from school and says she lost her lunch money for the umpteenth time. The temptation may be for you to rush to school with more money or a sandwich. Natural consequences should apply here—your daughter isn't going to starve from missing one meal. Unless there are medical reasons otherwise, let her learn from this event by telling her you are sorry, but you will have a light snack ready when she gets home from school. Until then, she must do without.

When my two boys were young, we had a schedule of chores that rotated from week to week. Sometimes there would be an argument between them about whose turn it was to feed the dog. I instituted a logical consequence. If the dog did not get fed by the evening meal, then the boy whose turn it was would not eat either. We had no more problems with that issue. The boys made very sure that Chex got her meal, even if they weren't sure whose turn it was.

Your child needs many opportunities to learn responsibility. The kinds of scenarios described in this section will need repeating. However, with a basic set of ideas on how to use these principles and strategies, you will be able to give your child a solid platform for learning to cope with behaviors related to attention-deficit.

It is crucial that you avoid reinforcing negative behaviors as much as possible. Ignore silly, inappropriate behaviors, and establish firm, consistent consequences for the more severe misbehaviors. Try as much as possible to plan your reaction ahead of time. Consistency and immediate enforcement are crucial, as is a calm but firm approach to the child's infractions.

Appropriate incentives, offering both rewards and punishments, are necessary. Time-out and grounding can be very useful, but be careful to adapt each tactic to the needs and age of your child. If you run into problems, consult with a psychologist or other professional.

Questions about Parental Intervention

1. What adjustments in discipline need to be made with adolescents who have ADHD?

By the time the typical ADHD child reaches adolescence, problems with attention span, impulsivity, and proneness to emotionality are often less pronounced than during childhood. But these problems remain, and may be expressed around issues such as the teenager's acceptance of responsibility—chores, homework, school performance, etc., disagreements over rights and privileges, and choices about friends and activities. The normal striving for independence which is typical for this stage is often intensified and heightened by the ADHD characteristics.

Teenagers frequently resist the behavioral management procedures that work for younger children. Strong consequences are needed. Grounding, loss of use of the car and allowances, and community service arrangements can be used, but consequences need to be short-lived so the teen isn't boxed in forever. The student needs to see light at the end of the tunnel. A teenager's ability to be patient is not very good at best, let alone when he has ADHD.

You may need to establish a core set of "bottom line" family rules which are not negotiable and which have serious consequences for violation. It may be necessary to reinforce your authority with external authority from the juvenile justice system or local police.

For the family with an ADHD adolescent, there are four major factors that influence the degree of trouble they may have as the teenager tries to individuate from his or her parents. These factors are: deficits in problem-solving and communication skills, cognitive distortions, family structure problems, and the biologically determined characteristics of ADHD—inattention, impulsivity, and hyperactivity. An intervention effort must evaluate the severity and nature of these issues for each family.

It is most helpful to get the family together and teach negotiation and contracting skills. It is important for the adolescent to feel as if his opinion matters and will be considered in the rule and decision-making process. It seldom does any good to force a passive resistant teenager to participate in treatment. The more directive approach found useful with younger ADHD children does not work as well with teenagers.[8]

2. What are signs of parental burnout and what can be done to prevent it?

Raising an ADHD child increases the chances of marital stress, but it probably does not cause parental or marriage burnout. Inherent problems in the marital relationship are intensified by coping with a difficult child. The addition of other stressors such as financial, occupational, emotional, or spiritual dysfunction will increase the likelihood of burnout, even in well-adjusted couples. When parents become so distraught they cannot function, it is a sign the entire support system has collapsed.

Signs of burnout include:

● A sudden or gradual, but sustained change in temperament of the parent. For example, a mild-mannered parent becomes consistently angry, argumentative, and critical.

● Your child no longer gives any sense of pleasure or joy. There is a sustained sense of frustration from being around him. You have a sense of futility about your efforts to change things, and a sense of helplessness about yourself as a parent and as a person.

● There is increasing fear that your anger will get out of control and you will hurt your child. You may have thoughts of violence, followed by guilt and remorse for having such thoughts. There is great fear or dread that your actions as a parent will cause significant psychological harm to your child.

● You have a strong sense of being alone in your struggles. No one understands, cares, or listens to your frustrations, and this creates an overwhelming feeling of overload.

Things you can do to deal with parental burnout include:

● Refresh your spiritual batteries. Go on a retreat, spend time with a spiritual mentor, attend a convention that is uplifting and positive. Ask for help. Let your pastor know about your struggles.

● Give attention to your relationship as a married couple. As important as your children are, the first priority is the health of the marriage. Plan ways to cultivate your life as a couple apart from the children. Spend time alone every week. Guard your time together. Have some fun. Do some things that uplift and refresh and which don't involve the children.

● Talk with your spouse about your concerns and frustrations, and keep talking. If you aren't married, talk to a trusted friend. Listen to each other's viewpoint. Learn how to be a safety valve for one another.

● While child-rearing is important, it is not the whole essence of who you are or what you do. Remember, your identity in Christ does not depend on performance or success, including parenting. Cultivate friends, interests, and activities that you can share with adults and as a couple.

● Find and use all the support systems available to you through your church, community groups, friends, parenting groups, and support groups such as CHADD. Meet other parents who are struggling with the same issues and learn from them.

● Learn to forgive yourself, your spouse, and your child for your collective and individual shortcomings. Keep your priorities in order. The better you care for your needs, the better parent you will be. Total and continual self-sacrifice is counterproductive to the entire family system.[9]

References

1. Garber, S.W., Garber, M.D., and Spizman, R.F., *If Your Child Is Hyperactive, Inattentive, Impulsive, Distractible . . . Helping the ADD Hyperactive Child* (New York: Villard Books, 1990).

2. Moss, R.A., *Why Johnny Can't Concentrate: Coping with Attention Deficit Problems* (New York: Bantam Books, 1990).

3. Barkley, R.A., *Cognitive-Behavioral Therapy with ADHD Children,* ed. Braswell, L., and Bloomquist, M.L. (New York:

The Guilford Press, 1991), vii–xi.

4. Attention-Deficit Disorders Association (ADDA), 8091 South Ireland Way, Aurora, CO 80016, (800)487-2282.

5. Challenge, "A Newsletter on Attention-Deficit Hyperactivity Disorder," P.O. Box 2001, West Newbury, MA 01985, (508)462-0495.

6. Children with Attention-Deficit Disorders (CHADD), National Headquarters, 499 N.W. 70th Avenue, Suite 308, Plantation, FL 33317, (305)587-3700.

7. Goldstein, S., and Goldstein, M., *Managing Attention Disorders in Children* (New York: John Wiley & Sons, 1990).

8. Robin, A.L., "Training Families with ADHD Adolescents," *Attention-Deficit Hyperactivity Disorder,* ed. Barkley, R.A. (New York: The Guilford Press, 1990), 462–97.

9. Adapted from material written by Rachel Goodman, appearing in Debra Maxey, *How to Own and Operate an Attention-Deficit Kid* (Roanoke, Virginia: HyperActive Attention Deficit [HAAD], P.O. Box 20563, Roanoke, VA 24018, 1989). Used by permisison of author.

10. Nadeau, K.G. and Dixon, E.B., *Learning to Slow Down and Pay Attention* (Annandale, Virginia: Chesapeake Psychological Services, 1991).

11. Adapted from Goldstein and Goldstein, *The Multi-Disciplinary Evaluation and Treatment of Children with Attention Deficit Disorders,* pages 72–73, Copyright 1991. Used by permission of authors and publisher.

12. Adapted from Goldstein and Goldstein, *Managing Attention Disorders in Children,* pages 360–362, Copyright 1990. Used by permission of authors and publisher.

13. Adapted from Goldstein and Goldstein, *Managing Attention Disorders in Children,* pages 362–363, Copyright 1990. Used by permission of authors and publisher.

ChAPTER FiVE

HOW CAN MY CHILD CHANGE?
Self-esteem and
Self-control Issues
for the ADHD Child

If you could give only one gift to your child, what would it be? Good health? Wealth? Perhaps it would be peace of mind or academic success. The Christian parent may quickly think about the gift of God's love in the person of Jesus Christ. A child's eternal destiny is of paramount importance, and a personal faith in Jesus Christ is an absolute necessity. After the spiritual dimension, most parents would want to give their child a good self-concept or proper self-esteem, for without this, he will never find happiness and contentment. There must be a basic foundation of having a realistic appraisal of oneself, accompanied by good feelings about who one is. This is self-esteem.

No one is born with self-esteem. It is learned day by day. Your child's sense of worth began the moment you first held him in your arms. That physical closeness provided your child with a sense of security. At ten minutes of age, the infant did not say to himself, "All right! This big person thinks I am special. I can tell by that smile on her face." But over time, as you cuddled him, fed him, responded to his cries, and cheered his first steps, he began to get the message. As each new skill was added to his repertoire, another dimension was added to his thoughts about himself.

Most children naturally grow up feeling good about themselves. But ADHD children have fewer successes, hear more no's, and face more rejection. As a result, their self-esteem is lower, and this carries into adulthood. Many of the specific sources of trouble and conflict will pass away as they leave their youth. How often does an adult have to sit still in a classroom with his hand raised, waiting for the teacher to ask a question? An adult can make excuses for some of his inattention or forgetfulness. But the residue of negative experiences, parental criticism, peer rejections, and failures of childhood remain. These feelings and thoughts continue to influence behavior long after the lunch box is stored away and the report cards are put in the attic.

Self-esteem or the way a person sees himself is an accumulation of many experiences. He may consider himself to be a good soccer player, a loyal friend, a poor speller, a mediocre reader, a great whistler, and a lousy brother. These all add up to some type of summary evaluation of who he is and how others see him.

The image one has of self is important because it gives a sense of fulfillment for the life that one lives. Self-esteem is essential to personal achievement, accomplishment, or value. A person with good self-esteem will be able to take risks. Some of those risks will result in more successes. These achievements, in turn, give the confidence to take more risks, to try more things, and can yield more positive feedback. However, for ADHD children, this cycle can work in reverse. They don't succeed, they develop less confidence, their judgment about themselves is low, and so they are less willing to try new things.

As you are learning about the nature of ADHD, the needs of your child should be coming more clearly into focus. It is my hope that you can be more systematic in helping your child accumulate more positive experiences on which to build a realistic positive opinion of himself. This section is intended to aid you in cultivating this important area in your child's life.

Notice my initial definition—a realistic appraisal of self accompanied by good feelings about who one is. Self-esteem is a cumulative opinion or judgment based on the feedback one receives throughout his lifetime. This total impression comes from many different experiences. To help you make sense of such a large concept, I am going to break self-esteem into four major categories—*security, belonging, competency, and purpose.* We'll discuss what each one means, along with ideas for enhancing the child's experiences within that area.

Sense of Security

Every child needs structure and limits set on behavior. The new infant needs to be wrapped in a blanket and held close to ensure bonding and health. As a child grows older, he desires more freedom. Yet, it must always be in the context of limits.

Imagine a single-lane highway bridging a river gorge. The narrow roadbed is suspended a thousand feet above the raging current and dangerous boulders below. There are even a few ferocious crocodiles and thousands of flesh-eating piranha just waiting for some type of food to fall from the bridge above.

You have to drive across this bridge. Unfortunately, it was constructed by the same people who built some of our downtown Seattle freeways. They were left unfinished—giant roadways in the sky with no access and abrupt endings; ribbons of concrete atop giant pillars, but going absolutely nowhere. Your bridge had the same contractor. There are no guard rails on this bridge—just a flat, one-lane surface with no warning markers. How would you approach the task of negotiating your way across this macabre bridge? My guess is that you would do it with extreme trepidation and considerable anxiety. Because there are no protective boundaries to the bridge, it is hard to tell where the relative safety of the road ends and the downward journey into the jaws of the crocodiles begins.

This bridge is a metaphor for the life of any child. But let's complicate the picture a bit. Suppose you have to drive across this bridge in a high-powered sports car. Even more problematic, the car's accelerator has a mind of its own. Sometimes the engine roars to life and wants to go a hundred miles an hour. Also, the brakes are very unreliable and may or may not work properly. Such an unpredictable car would be a challenge in itself, without having to negotiate this bridge of horrors. Such is the experience of your ADHD child.

• Self-esteem can be aided by establishing guidelines and limits. Your child's sense of security is enhanced by knowing exactly what is expected of him and by experiencing consistent consequences for keeping or breaking those limits. All of the ideas presented in chapter 4 will contribute to this aspect of self-esteem. Parents should strive for reasonable consistency in enforcing rules and avoid unexpected enforcement. ADHD children don't handle change very well, and they will be more erratic when faced with new requirements without prior notice.

• Consistent enforcement of positive and negative consequences is more important than severity. Regular use of five minutes of time-out, for example, will be more effective than intermittent corporal punishment.

The use of positive reinforcement is very important in building a child's self-image. Punishment is necessary, and you need to learn how to use it effectively. We have looked at various forms already. A key concept here is to make sure there are more positive, reinforcing events than negative ones. I would suggest you try to *give your child at least four positive exchanges for every negative one. Eight to one would be even better.* These do not have to be material rewards. Quite the contrary. Hugs, compliments, mutual activities, shared jokes, laughter, common interests, and private moments together are examples of positive exchanges.

A relationship with your child can be seen as a *savings account* at the bank. You have to make deposits in that account for it to have any value. At some point, it is inevitable you will have to make withdrawals too. But if you withdraw without making deposits, the account will eventually be depleted. Your relationship with that account comes to an end.

The same is true with your child. You made many early deposits when your child was an infant. But as he grew older, it became necessary to discipline and make some withdrawals from that account. You need to make sure you keep ahead of the balance sheet. The *four to one positive ratio* will help you do that.

• Trust is another aspect of your child's sense of security. An ADHD child needs to know the significant adults around him can be depended upon to do what they say. It is important to keep your promises. Don't make idle statements about possibly going to the zoo unless you intend to do so. Keep this kind of verbal brainstorming to yourselves. Once your child hears about it, in his mind it is already happening.

On the other side of the coin, don't make threats about restrictions, groundings, time-outs, or other forms of punishment. If these are needed, impose them immediately. Don't just get emotional and rant and rave. (Do that in the privacy of your bedroom, support group, or in the soundproof laundry room.)

Imagine a traffic cop whose job it is to make frustrated and irritable drivers obey the speed limit. The problem is that this particular policeman only has his whistle. So he valiantly stands on the sidewalk, looking sternly at each passing speeder, and blowing his whistle as loudly as possible. While this may startle the drivers upon first seeing the man in blue with the red face and puffy cheeks, the long-term effect is quite predictable. With no ability to enforce or apply consequences, the policeman is powerless to slow people down. The same is true of the parent who makes threats and seldom follows through. This does nothing to build your child's sense of security.

Sense of Belonging

The next important component of self-esteem is the child's awareness of belonging and of being a meaningful member of a family. Your child needs to know he is a part of a unit of humans who care for one another, have a common heritage, and aspire to common goals. Individual meaning and value is gained because of this perception of participation and identity.

This could be called a sense of family or community. The child needs to know his home is a place where he can be safe, no matter what happens in the outside world.

Plan family activities that build this feeling of belonging and that strengthen an awareness of fun, unity, and unique identity. Appreciation of your family name and your unique heritage is important. Contact with extended family helps tremendously, assuming that the relationships are positive. Hearing stories about grandparents, family histories, and traditions all give a child an appreciation for what has gone before, and how he is a part of the ongoing family line. Continue important traditions that reflect your family culture and religious beliefs. Also find ways to include your child in the planning and expression of these traditions. *Building memories* around the family unit is important.

Individual activities such as creating a family crest, making a picture collage, or designing a family banner can be used to identify and express the various elements of your family identity. Participation in the design and decoration of the family home and individual rooms can also help. Encourage the expression of the inclusive "we" in discussions relating to family activities, needs, and interests, instead of the exclusive "I."

Avoid highly competitive games with your ADHD child. Often he can't be successful, so don't expose him to additional frustration and failure with intense games of Scrabble or Monopoly. Your child probably wouldn't have the patience to sit through such a game anyway. Also be careful about academic, artistic, musical, or athletic comparisons. Differences in abilities are inevitable. Just do the best you can to highlight successes. Encourage cooperation and mutual problem-solving, rather than wins and losses. Ridicule and teasing should be minimized. Playful joking is fine, but do all you can to keep mean and cruel statements to a minimum.

Responsibilities are an important part of belonging to a family unit. Teach respect for property and personal space. If each child has a room, bed, closet, or box, they should be able to exercise control over who has access to that space. See that each child respects the rights of others, as well as receives reciprocal respect from other family members. Shared chores and mutual responsibility for the physical condition of the house and related property should be encouraged. Children usually can't be responsible for major chores or house repair, but activities should be identified that fit the skills of each child, including your ADHD child. He needs to be part of a team effort and to have that effort recognized and praised.

As your child grows older, outside groups will take on increased importance. Sports teams, music groups, clubs, classes, and friendship groups will be additional places where your child can have a sense of belonging. We know, of course, that many ADHD children have trouble fitting into these groups, due to their impetuous and awkward style. This only serves to highlight the importance of making the family unit a comfortable, warm environment in which to belong.

There is one additional crucial element to our sense of belonging. It is found in our identity as children of God. We will discuss this later.

Sense of Competency

Nothing helps build a child's confidence faster than large doses of success. Your child gains a sense of competency as those closest to him are able to affirm his uniqueness. Those abilities, interests, personality traits, and learning styles all go together to make each person a special creation. Our culture tends to emphasize intelligence, physical beauty, and material possessions. If your child has these attributes, your task may be easier. However, the ADHD child needs a balance of feedback that recognizes his hidden, as well as conspicuous, strengths.

The many ideas for skill-building and compliance-training which are discussed in this and other chapters all contribute to your child's assessment of competence. All of this fits together to build up self-esteem. It is very easy for an ADHD child to fall into the habit of "nothing ventured, nothing lost." If he believes most of his choices or actions will result in failure, he won't try. Your goal is to help him improve his skills so that he will more often be successful. In addition, you want to discover ways to help him compensate for weak areas by using his strengths.

I have an ADHD client who, when he first came to see me, was struggling with his homework and had no friends at school. He is very bright, but tends to talk a mile a minute. Usually he doesn't give his classmates a chance to get a word in edgewise. He has many skills to draw on, but as I was doing some assessment in the early stages I found out he has an incredible visual memory. Besides the formal test results I found confirmation of this strength while playing the card game called "Concentration." The game is played by randomly laying rows of cards facedown on the table. You take turns examining each card, one at a time, and then try to remember where each half of the pair is located. If you turn up a red Anger card (I used special feeling cards), you can keep it *if* you can also turn up its complementary card. Your turn is over if you guess at the wrong card.

Playing against this fourth-grade boy, I lost 25 to 2. I couldn't believe how he could remember the location of each card once he had examined it. I mentioned this to his mom and she confirmed his fantastic skill in this area. I am now trying to draw on his visual memory skills as we look for ways to control his excessive talking. He uses pictures we create in counseling sessions to help remind himself to slow down, look at the bored expressions of his peers, and tell himself to "stop." This is an example of *using a strength to compensate for a weakness.* It is a vital tool for building competency.

One of the most important ways a parent can encourage a child's striving toward competency is through *unconditional love.* I have mentioned several times how an ADHD child usually has a history of criticism, failure, and rejection. Your child needs large doses of love and affirmation with no strings attached.

The self-rating scale allows you to take a close-up view of how you are doing in regard to the sacrificial love described in 1 Corinthians 13. Don't be too hard on yourself—nobody but the Lord could score a perfect ten on everything. Use this as a way to examine yourself and establish some goals for areas of improvement in your family, and particularly for your ADHD child.

HOW DO I OFFER THE GIFT OF LOVE?

Love is patient, love is kind. It does not envy, it does not boast, it is not proud. It is not rude, it is not self-seeking, it is not easily angered, it keeps no record of wrongs. Love does not delight in evil but rejoices with the truth. It always protects, always trusts, always hopes, always perseveres. 1 Corinthians 13:4-7

Considering the scriptural definition of *agape* love, rank yourself on a scale of 1–10 (1=very weak, 10=very strong). Circle one number for each description.

LOVE IS PATIENT: I am slow to get angry with the ones I love. I do not yell or lose my temper. I can hang in there, no matter what happens.	1 2 3 4 5 6 7 8 9 10
LOVE IS KIND: I am thoughtful, generous in my praise, always looking for ways to uplift others.	1 2 3 4 5 6 7 8 9 10
LOVE DOES NOT ENVY: I am not jealous of the successes of others. I don't pout or pick flaws.	1 2 3 4 5 6 7 8 9 10
LOVE DOESN'T BOAST: I don't hog the conversation, or exaggerate the facts to make an impression.	1 2 3 4 5 6 7 8 9 10
LOVE ISN'T CONCEITED: I don't harbor an inflated view of my importance. I don't twist the conversation to draw attention to myself.	1 2 3 4 5 6 7 8 9 10
LOVE ISN'T RUDE: I'm not cruel, crude, or cutting, but am polite, courteous, and complimentary.	1 2 3 4 5 6 7 8 9 10
LOVE ISN'T SELFISH: I'm not self-centered, making others fit into my mold, or setting expectations on others for my own interests. I'm not possessive of others, nor do I insist on my own way.	1 2 3 4 5 6 7 8 9 10
LOVE ISN'T EASILY ANGERED: I'm not touchy, cranky, defensive, brittle, or supersensitive.	1 2 3 4 5 6 7 8 9 10
LOVE KEEPS NO RECORD OF WRONGS: I'm able to forgive. I don't have to seek revenge, retaliate, or defend myself when hurt.	1 2 3 4 5 6 7 8 9 10
LOVE DOESN'T GLOAT OVER THE SINS OF OTHERS: I don't rejoice when others are proven wrong. I don't take pleasure in reminding others of their faults or by saying, "I told you so."	1 2 3 4 5 6 7 8 9 10
LOVE REJOICES IN TRUTH: I'm glad when right and justice prevail, no matter who gets the credit. I'm strong in my convictions but leave room for my own error. I'm happy when others succeed.	1 2 3 4 5 6 7 8 9 10

Sense of Purpose

A sense of purpose gives *direction* for our lives. Direction is crucial, for if we don't know where we are going, we will get lost. Knowing our purpose under God gives us a compass bearing. The spiritual instructions you give to your child should respond to the question, "Why am I here?" A child doesn't need a detailed course in theology, but he does need continual exposure to those values and concepts that give meaning and purpose to life. These concepts are taught over many years. There will be formal times of instruction, such as during family devotions. There will be informal instruction when your child asks a specific question such as, "Dad, why are we Christians?"

The Bible tells us that God has given humankind the task of subduing and ruling over the earth as His representatives (Psalm 8:6). We are here to be of service to God. We are called to worship and honor our Creator (1 Chronicles 16:29; Psalm 95:6). We are asked to be wise and good stewards over creation (Luke 19:13ff; Romans 14:12).

As children of God our purpose includes enjoying fellowship with our Father (Psalms 34:18; 145:18; Acts 17:27). Our calling is to be God's representatives on earth. As stewards of all that He created, we have the major purpose of *bearing fruit* (John 15:16). As we use our abilities and gifts in service to others, the fruit of love, joy, peace, patience, kindness, goodness, faithfulness, gentleness, and self-control will be nourished and multiplied in us (Galatians 5:22-23).

To bear fruit, then, becomes our response to the nagging question of, "Why do we exist?" We can know that God placed us here. Living a life of faith can give us a solid sense of purpose. As we focus on the maturation process, knowing our labors are to result in love, joy, peace, we will be better able to keep on course and fulfill our destiny.

There are many ways to apply these concepts to your child. First, you need to know and claim them for your own life. Once that is in process, the fruit will begin to show and touch the life of your child. Your goal is to teach and model a life of faith and reliance on God. As your child sees that faith result in patience, even in times of crisis and stress, he is learning valuable lessons about drawing on God's resources. I will say more about this in chapter 8.

The other key component of teaching our children a sense of purpose is our *identity* as children of God. We need to do everything we can to expose our children to the biblical evidence of our individual worth. We were fearfully and wonderfully made (Psalm 139:13-16). We are products of God's workmanship (Ephesians 2:10). We are created in the image of God and His likeness resides within us (Genesis 1:27). He doesn't look at us, see our imperfections, and say, "I've made a mistake here. I'd better try again."

God values us enough that He seeks our worship (John 4:23). Christ, His Son, accepts us as we are—with no strings attached (John 6:37). We are precious in God's eyes (Isaiah 43:4). We are important enough to God that He allowed the death of His Son for our redemption (1 Peter 1:18-19). Further, we have been adopted by God and made His sons and daughters (Romans 8:14-17). We are children of the King (1 John 3:1).

These promises and descriptions define who we are in a spiritual sense. They are the *facts* of our existence. While we may not always feel like they are true, these are the basic cornerstones on which we can claim to have a solid identity or self-esteem. Belonging, security, and success are human requirements. But the basis of our ability to look past the problems of an ADHD child rests in our rights as children of God.

Methods of Teaching Self-Control and Attention

Often the only thing most ADHD children know about being still is what their parents tell them. "Joey, sit still." "Joey, I've told you a dozen times to be quiet. Now do it." While other children can sit through a meal without incident, an ADHD child will wiggle, rock, and squirm his way from appetizer to dessert.

Recently a teacher told me of an ADHD student in another classroom who tries very hard to sit still but has major difficulty doing so. (His mother won't have anything to do with medication or any other formal form of intervention.) Larry's class was having a special speaker, and Larry knew if he caused any distractions he would get a detention. Later he told the teacher what happened. While listening to the speaker, Larry noticed his hands were moving all around. So, to get them under control, he sat on them. But after a while, he noticed his feet were bouncing all around his desk. To keep his feet still he wrapped his feet around the legs of his chair. This might have worked, except after a few more minutes in this awkward position, his body started moving and he and his chair tipped over, causing a major disturbance. He still got a detention, in spite of his heroic efforts to avoid it.

An ADHD child must learn to take control of his reactions. He can become less active and filter out distractions. In this section I will share some ways you can help your child control his movement, set the idle lower, and put a limit on his impulses. This takes specific training. Other children naturally turn their motion on and off. They can consciously focus attention and resist the urge to move around. Your ADHD youngster must learn how to do this. In examining many resources, I have found the book, *If Your Child Is Hyperactive, Inattentive, Impulsive, Distractible ... Helping the ADD/Hyperactive Child*, to be extremely helpful in teaching these skills. I will draw from this book in summarizing the following games and activities.[1]

● *Statue.* This is the first step in teaching your child how to gain control over his body. You will need a stopwatch and a chart to display progress. The goal of this game is to learn to sit perfectly still for an increasing amount of time.

After discussing with your child his need to learn to sit still, teach him how to pose like a statue. Show him pictures of statues and practice striking various poses, like the palace guard or the Statue of Liberty. Take turns creating these different statues.

Then help your child become more aware of his impulses by playing Catch Me If You Can. Sit in chairs opposite one another with your feet comfortably touching the floor. Tell your child to watch you carefully and catch any movement you make, aside from breathing and slight changes in facial expression or eyes. Exaggerate your movements initially, and then become more subtle, giving your child a chance to see the differences. Then reverse roles so you can point out his obvious violations. Be positive so that the fun aspect of the game is highlighted. Encourage awareness of how stillness feels, as well as the urge to move. Have him close his eyes and concentrate on various muscle groups. Work toward discriminating tense from relaxed muscles. He will need this ability later with other self-control techniques.

Now you start the game of World Records. Have your child set a reasonable and attainable goal for how long he can stay perfectly still like a statue. Then begin timing these trials. When he sets a new record, record it on a chart. Points can be given for reaching certain levels. Proceed slowly. Each additional second is another success. Praise his progress. Avoid long practice sessions. Keep it fun, and stop while he is still enthused. Repeat the game every several days, and continue until he can sit still for five minutes fairly consistently.

• *Beat the Clock.* The Statue game is the first step in your child's efforts to control his activity level. The next step is to begin extending this skill to other situations. Beat the Clock helps your child learn how to match his body motion to the requirements of various situations. Each place you go has its own unspoken set of rules. Most of us learn these rules by watching others and refining our skills through feedback. The ADHD child requires a more direct form of instruction.

Begin by selecting your target situation. A good idea might be dinnertime at home. Later you could work on church services, Sunday School, or a meal at a pizza parlor. Develop a set of realistic rules with your child. Ask these questions: What kind of behavior is appropriate? How are other people behaving in the situation? What cues are available that tell us how to act?

Construct statements that describe reasonable behavior for the situation. The rules should be stated positively. Use your child's words to describe the desired behavior. The rules should reflect minimum standards in the beginning. You will work with approximations at the outset. Later the rules can be refined.

Don't allow too many rules to be listed. Also keep the

statements positive and as simple as possible. A discussion of the dinner hour might result in the following rules:

1. Stay at the table until you are given permission to leave.
2. Sit with your bottom on the chair and your feet on the floor.
3. Use silverware to eat.

Write the rules on a clock card like Figure 5.1. This has been adapted from cards in Garber, Garber, and Spizman.[1] Start with the general goal of remaining at the table for a meal. Before you actually play the game at mealtime, give it a run-through in a quiet setting with few distractions. Use a stopwatch or a timer with a second hand, and role play the rules, beginning with number 1. Demonstrate correct and incorrect ways to obey each rule. Time each attempt and call time when a rule is clearly violated. Record the progress on the card. Another chart can be made to keep track of points. The child receives one point for equaling a previous time and two points for setting a new record.

The next step is to play the Beat the Clock game in a real setting. Play the game one time to set the initial time goal. In subsequent trials, the game begins with the last goal achieved. Keep the atmosphere light and positive. It is good to give time cues during the game. Statements such as, "You've made it to five minutes so far. You only have two more to go," will help keep the child on target. Review the clock cards at the end of each session and total the points and transfer them to his point total chart. You could use beans or marbles in a jar to keep track of his points.

As his behavior improves, gradually add more rules. New challenges are a sign of progress. Write the new rules on the clock card, but remember, "Small steps for little feet." Don't make the new rules too big of an improvement over the previous ones.

The final steps involve trying the game outside the home. Pick situations which have the best chance of success, and keep the setting as simple as possible. Use the clock card to monitor success. You might also develop silent hand or facial signals to help prompt your child as you go along. These

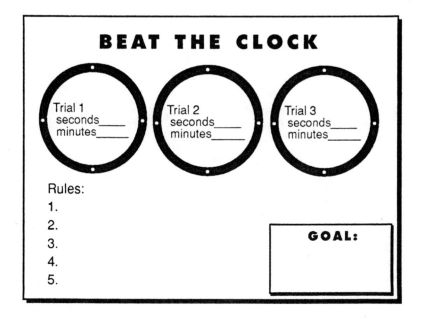

signals can be very helpful in a public setting. Remember to heap on the praise.

● *Endurance Training.* Your child first learned he could control his activity level with Statue. With Beat the Clock he learned there are particular behaviors that are appropriate for different situations. With Endurance Training you are going for the long haul. The goal is to strengthen the skills and stretch the time your child is able to sit still in a variety of settings.

Think about the places where your child has the most difficulty behaving appropriately. Such a list may include: church services, riding in the car, movies, music lessons, and restaurants.

Talk with your child about the appropriate behaviors for the first setting. Define the rules for this situation. List them on the card, and set an endurance goal. In this case, it would be sitting through an entire church service. In Beat the Clock the goals were based on time—five minutes, twenty-five minutes, etc. But the real world doesn't always follow the clock exactly. With Endurance Training, the time frame is matched to the setting. In our example, most children can sit through an entire church service.

One key to achieving this goal is to divide the situation into manageable parts. It's probably not reasonable to expect your child to make it through the entire service, and so you divide the situation into segments. These time goals might be: *First,* sit in the service until the singing is done. *Second,* sit through the service until the sermon starts. *Third,* sit through the service until the sermon is finished. *Last,* sit through the entire service.

After the goals are determined and behaviors are practiced, it is time to try everything in the real setting. Set a goal for the first attempt. In this example it would be to sit still until the singing is over. When the goal is reached, mark it on the clock face and praise his success. Since you will need to leave in the middle for a few weeks, you will be missing portions of the worship service yourself. However, the investment in your child's increased ability to make it through a service without you tearing out your hair will pay off later. Maybe Mom and Dad can take turns leaving the service. And be sure you don't make the premature leaving too rewarding. Stopping at McDonald's on the way home is not appropriate if the child did not reach his goal. Points can be earned as before. If the goal is found to be hard to achieve, divide it into smaller segments, and try again. Clear-cut misbehavior can be handled with a two-point fine. Continued violations could result in a time-out.[1]

Continue the Endurance Training as long as needed. Keep the pace reasonable: it may take longer, but the benefits are clearly worth every effort you put into it.

● *Calmness Training.* As we well know, an ADHD child does not handle the unexpected very well. Transitions pose an ongoing obstacle because the child tends to become overexcited. If he is tired, the results are even more problematic. He is more susceptible to overarousal and less able to be attentive.

Calmness training or relaxation offers a partial solution to these problems. This technique provides a skill that can be taken anywhere. It can help your child fall asleep, reduce his fear of new situations, keep calm during an argument, and even be in a better state of mind before taking a test.

Relaxation is not a form of self-hypnosis. It is simply a method of progressive flexing and relaxing of each muscle group in the body until the person is more calm and relaxed. Basically, it consists of measured breathing and muscle relaxation. It is a biological process. It is not supernatural in any way unless one contaminates it with various mystical beliefs and practices. All we are going to do is get the muscles to relax and the child to think about positive, calming events.

The Statue game is a good prerequisite for this, because it has taught the child how to sit still for a short period of time. Now we can add to that skill by teaching the body how to be more comfortable. Remember, this is a skill that takes repeated practice. Your child may not immediately recognize the value of this training. Some rewards may be necessary to get him to cooperate and continue.

Have your child sit in a comfortable chair or sofa. His feet should be on the floor and the back of his head should be able to rest on the top of the chair. His arms should rest easily by his sides, the palms of his hands lying on the seat. Sit opposite the child so he can see and mirror your activity. When he is in position, ask him to freeze for a short time. Praise this effort and offer the prospect of more rewards if necessary.

Begin by making a big wide yawn with your mouth wide open, your eyes squeezed tightly shut, and your nose wrinkled. Hold this position for a few seconds, inhale deeply through your mouth, and then suddenly exhale and sigh, almost closing your mouth so it remains only slightly open and relaxed. Do this a few times and ask your child to repeat the yawning routine. Praise his cooperation, administer points as needed, and remember to practice at various times, such as sitting at the dinner table or while riding in the car.

The next step is to teach diaphragm breathing. Here you place one hand, palm down, over your belly button. Take big, slow breaths that fill the abdomen with air. As you slowly breathe in to the count of five, your abdomen should rise as it inflates with air. As you exhale, your stomach should sink.

You want to produce full, easy breaths at the rate of about five seconds in and five seconds out. Your goal is four to six inhale-exhale cycles a minute.

Have your child copy your actions and give him constructive feedback and praise. Combine the big yawn with the breathing. Practice this routine for several minutes. Use a timer to indicate when your child has reached his goal.

Another feature to the relaxation is to think about words such as "calm," "relaxed," "still," and "peaceful." The child could also think about a favorite place, such as the beach or a mountain lake. Help him recall what it feels like to be floating on a raft or lying on the warm sand. I have asked older children to think about favorite Bible verses or the words to a hymn or Scripture song.

The next step in the sequence is to continue the relaxed deep breathing and systematically tense and relax your body, starting with your arms and hands. Clinch your fists, flex your arms, and then relax them completely. Do this for each side of the body, and repeat it three times. Have your child copy your actions, and help him focus on the difference between the tense and relaxed state. After the hands and arms, you can move to the legs and feet. Tense each by tightening the muscles on the back of your calf and your foot by pulling your toes back toward your body. (If you are susceptible to any kind of muscle spasms or back problems, be sure to check these activities with your doctor.)

Lead your child through this entire sequence several times. You might even make a tape with instructions paced for each activity. Background music can fill in the practice times. The advantage of the tape is that the child can use it to practice when you aren't around. This also helps him accept responsibility for his learning. You can promote this kind of initiative through verbal praise and handing out bonus points.

Continued daily practice is essential to make this skill a useful part of your child's life. The more you practice, the more automatic it will become. Encourage your child to try relaxation several times a day. You might want to make a chart that monitors the number of daily or weekly practice sessions. Bonus points can be given for beating last week's practice total. Always make sure the practice is of sufficient quality and duration to be of value.

Try out ways to apply the calmness techniques while sitting in the car or in other public places. Make a game of seeing if you and your child can practice without others knowing. Yawning and deep breathing will be easy to do. Tensing and relaxing the various muscle groups may not be possible to conceal, unless you have refined the techniques so that a more simple form of tension is sufficient. An example is to tense up the stomach muscles and then relax them. This can be done without obvious external body movement. Remember, *you* are going to gain from this technique also. Each of you can realize benefits as relaxation is applied to school, home, and social situations.[1]

• *Impulse Control Training.* Impulsiveness is one of the main reasons ADHD children end up with injuries and accidents. It may change its form over the lifespan, but ADHD youngsters do not simply outgrow this characteristic. Therefore, it is crucial to teach your child to regulate his impulses better. The goal here is to stop and think before acting.

Start by having a quiet discussion of impulsiveness. Use examples of when your child acted rashly and compare those to situations when it was evident he had stopped to deliberate. Make a list of impulsive acts and thought-out acts, as in Figure 5.2.

Impulsive Acts	Thought-Out Acts
Running into the street	Pausing at light or curb and looking both ways
Leaving house without schoolbooks	Putting books in book bag when homework is done
Interrupting conversations	Saying, "Excuse me," and waiting to speak
Grabbing toy from little brother	Asking to play with a toy
Pushing in line	Waiting for a turn

Figure 5.2 *Impulsive versus Thinking Behavior*[1]

Continue the discussion and examine the consequences of each action. Speculate on what would have happened if he had acted more prudently. Expand your list to look like Figure 5.3. This exercise will help your child understand that impulsiveness is related to acting without thinking, as well as to acting quickly. It is instructive to examine the negative consequences, along with the more positive outcomes from stopping to think first. This will help your child see the wisdom in learning to lessen his impulsiveness.

Impulsive Acts	Negative Consequences	Alternative If Thought First
Leaving home-work at home	Redo work	Free time at school
Running into street	Hit by car	Safe crossing
Blurting out	Not called on/ reprimanded	Answer question/ good grade
Grabbing toy	Lose toy	Play with toy

Figure 5.3 *Impulsive Acts and Consequences*[1]

Once your child understands the concept of impulsive behavior and the nature of negative consequences, you are ready to pinpoint those aspects of his behavior you want to change. Go over all the situations you can think of and identify those priority behaviors that need attention. This list will be your guide for the next step.

To be able to think before acting, your child will have to lengthen the time between impulse and action. To do this, he must learn to *hesitate* between thought and deed. Begin with the highest priority on your list and simulate the natural circumstances as closely as possible. If pausing before crossing the street is your goal, then actually go to the street. Practice stopping, looking both ways, and thinking about this step before crossing. Supervise closely before letting him try the hesitation response on his own. Give lots of feedback and praise. Keep it positive so that he doesn't get discouraged.

Each situation on your list will require a different hesitation response. Keep it simple and practical. Before leaving the house, your child may need to take one step backward and check himself from head to toe to see if he has left anything behind. You might use visual cues to help him remind himself of the need to stop and think. For example, a red dot on the front door might do the trick.

I implemented this idea with a boy who often forgot his lunch money, book bag, homework, schoolbooks, and musical instrument. He and his mother constructed a red stop sign with a list of symbols for each of the items to remember. Before going out the door David is to stop, review the list, and check himself to see if everything is accounted for.

You might make cards like the clock cards used earlier, but with a place to record the behavior your child is working on and the specific hesitation response he is going to use to achieve control. Your child will need many opportunities to practice this behavior. Rehearsal is crucial. Mastery takes practice. The hesitation response must become ingrained. You will need to work on it over and over.

When you see your child using his stop-and-think skill, give him lots of praise. There will be times when he will still act impulsively. To help the process, you need to correct impulsive behavior when it occurs. This is a time to use positive practice and overcorrection as described earlier.

When a child demonstrates mastery of a particular situation over a period of several weeks, make a big deal out of his accomplishment. Keep an ongoing record of the stop-and-think situations. Plan victory celebrations. If the initial list is mastered, have a type of graduation ceremony before creating a new and more sophisticated list. The schooling never ends, but the gradual improvements are worth every bit of effort.

• *Beating Distractions.* A pencil falls on the floor. Some students ignore it completely. Others look around to see who dropped it and immediately go back to work. An ADHD student will stop working on his spelling words, look at the source of the noise, giggle at the novelty of the event, reach in his desk to find the hyperspace special green pencil he has in reserve if he should ever drop his pencil, take it out, examine the small spaceships painted on the pencil, and then begin daydreaming about flying in outer space. A simple distraction has caused this child to totally forget about his spelling words—until his teacher brings him back on task.

A zillion distractions are out there waiting to snag the attention of every ADHD child. A short walk to his bedroom to get his coat can be like picking his way through a minefield. Every sight and sound is a possible temptation to draw his attention away from the original goal. The ADHD child has a natural inability to filter out competing stimuli. It's like the difficulty you might have if you were trying to find an error in your checkbook while standing in the middle of Grand Central Station at rush hour.

Teaching your child to ignore distractions is difficult, but not impossible. It takes lots of effort and practice. Yet progress can be made on this crucial skill. The process consists, first, in identifying those things that are most distracting for your child. Second, you teach him how to use a distraction zapper. Finally, you help him practice this technique in play and then in settings that demand high concentration.

Begin this effort by making a list of distractions to help your child become aware of his specific distractions. Work together like a couple of detectives to accumulate this list. Is your child more sensitive to visual or verbal stimuli? Some will be distracted by various combinations. What about internal thoughts, feelings, or body functions or sensations? You might make a picture to illustrate the intensity of the different visual, auditory, or internal stimuli. A graph or speedometer type of visual aid would work.

Next, you teach him to ignore the various stimuli by introducing the idea of *distraction zapping*. Young children, particularly boys, like action zappers like ray guns, laser rays, or phaser guns. Other possibilities are superman breath, disappearing blink, finger snap, finger point, or helpful wand. Having fun with this idea is very important. With the zapper firmly in hand, the child can now proceed to walk up the stairs to get his coat, cheerfully zapping every potential distractor in sight. You have now made a game out of avoiding being snagged by those ornery distractions lying in wait along the pathway. Make clear that this is a method to help the child stay on task. It is not just a game to use when everything else gets boring. Although enjoyable, this activity is very purposeful.

From simple play, build activities where your child can easily zap various distractions and be loud and dramatic in the process. Then move to more crucial activities such as homework. Start with events in the home, and after reaching some success, apply the zapper to more public situations such as the classroom. In the beginning, the zapper may be boisterous and even aggressive. Usually, the technique becomes more subdued and private after a few weeks.

Again, practice makes perfect. Create situations where distractions abound. Make up audio tapes and play them while your child is trying to concentrate on something. Make up a point system for success in these training sessions. Create a master list of items that no longer hold the power of distraction. Give lots of praise for honest additions to that list. Provide surprise rewards when your child uses this new skill in natural settings.

Don't expect perfection. All of us are diverted once in a while. One of the keys here is giving the child another form of control over his life. He is more able to tune out distractions, and choose to stay on task with greater authority and ease.

This concludes our discussion of tools and skills parents can share with their ADHD child to help with the problems of activity level, impulsivity, and distractibility. Many of the books listed in the resource section include other ideas. These techniques address the problematic features of ADHD. They take lots of work and a great deal of practice. The benefits are gradual, but definitely worth the effort.

Questions about Self-Control and Social Skills

1. *Why do parents have to work so hard at incorporating these skills into the life of an ADHD child? Won't medication take care of most of the problems?*

Stimulant medication is certainly a common treatment strategy in the clinical management of ADHD children. But there are problems and limitations with looking to medication as the singular intervention.

First of all, as many as 20 or 30 percent of ADHD children may not respond favorably to medication. Either there is no improvement or there are significant negative side effects that rule out continued usage.

A second reason for looking to other forms of intervention is the need for both the parents and child to learn new and improved methods of handling their interactions. Even if medication is helpful, the child is going to have times of noncompliance. Years of negative experience have left all members of the family with bad habits which they need to overcome.

Third, during times when medication is not taken, the child and parents need to rely on other means of handling their behavioral difficulties. Evenings, weekends, and vacation periods are often designated as drug-free holidays. These can be times of major emotional and behavioral setback if improved management and behavioral changes are not in place.

A fourth area of concern is the social arena of an ADHD child's life. Usually there have been problems in making and keeping friends, getting along with teachers, and social skills. The child needs help in learning the self-control and socialization skills that have been missing to this point.

For these reasons a program to encourage these skills and behaviors is recommended. The parent may receive assistance from outside professions for ideas, content, and procedures. However, the parent is the one constant in bringing about permanent improvements in the behavior of the ADHD child.

2. *What is meant by self-control training? What is the basic purpose in teaching this set of skills?*

A program teaching self-control will usually include material to teach children to:

- inhibit responding or to stop and think,
- repeat the problem or instruction,
- describe the nature of the problem,
- describe possible alternative approaches to the problem,
- evaluate the possible consequences of each alternative,

- undertake the problem solution while engaging in self-instructed guidance, and
- evaluate their own performance.[2]

Self-control is thought to proceed through three stages of development in most children. In the first stage, their behavior is controlled by outside events, primarily by the parents. In the second stage, children learn to control their own behavior to some degree. But they still require some type of self-generated external direction (self-talk) as a means of initiating and following through with appropriate behavior. By the third stage, children develop the ability to move through the problem-solving process more automatically. They are not so dependent on outside sources to direct their behavior. As a result their behavior is more self-controlled through a covert, unobserved process.

ADHD children do not seem to learn this process through "normal" experience and often need specific instruction on how to do it. Parents are very important in teaching these skills. Research has shown that instruction in self-control does not generalize outside of a class unless the child's caretakers (parents and teachers) are very involved in the effort.

3. *What is social-skills training for ADHD children?*

The majority of ADHD children experience either social incompetence or aggression, or both. While medication has been shown to be effective in reducing aggressive behavior, a component of social-skills training is essential for the ADHD child having problems in these areas. Two of the major goals of social-skills training are that the ADHD child will become more knowledgeable about appropriate and inappropriate social behavior, and will learn the specific social skills targeted and identified during the assessment process.

There is quite a bit of overlap between social-skills training and the self-control training described earlier. Most programs seem to focus on four major skill areas: social entry, conversational skills, conflict resolution and problem-solving, and anger management.[3]

One particular program teaches twenty-one specific social skills. These skills include: listening; meeting new people; introducing others; conversations; ending a conversation; rewarding self; asking a question; asking a favor; asking for help with a problem; following instructions; sharing; interpreting body language; playing a game; suggesting an activity; working cooperatively; offering to help; saying thank you; giving a compliment; accepting a compliment; apologizing; understanding the impact your behavior has on others; and demonstrating the ability to understand the behavior of others.[4]

The major theme that emerges from the evaluation of both self-control and social-skill training efforts for ADHD children is the need for active and comprehensive parental involvement. The content of either of these programs will have little effect unless there is involvement from the natural change agents in the child's life. These include the people closest to the child—parents, close relatives, teachers, and classmates.

References

1. Garber, S.W., Garber, M.D., and Spizman, R.F., *If Your Child Is Hyperactive, Inattentive, Impulsive, Distractible . . . Helping the ADD Hyperactive Child* (New York: Villard Books, 1990).

2. Kendall, P.C., and Braswell, L., *Cognitive-Behavioral Therapy for Impulsive Children* (New York: The Guilford Press, 1985).

3. Barkley, R.A., *Attention-Deficit Hyperactivity Disorder, A Handbook for Diagnosis and Treatment* (New York: The Guilford Press, 1990).

4. Goldstein, S., and Pollock, E., *Social Skills Training for Attention-Deficit Children* (Salt Lake City: Neurology, Learning and Behavior Center, 1988).

ChAPTER SiX

HOW CAN THE PHYSICIAN HELP?
Medical Treatment for
the ADHD Child

Jeff and Julie had just returned from the second planning session with Dr. Howard. As they had discussed several intervention strategies for their son, Danny, the doctor raised the question of medication as something Danny's parents should consider.

"I just don't know whether I want to give Danny medication," Jeff said.

"Yes, I agree," replied Julie, "but I think we should at least weigh the pros and cons. If it can help his brain to function better, maybe it's worth trying."

"But what if it stunts his growth, or causes him to be dependent on drugs when he's older?" asked Jeff. "I'd hate to give him something that seemed to help for now, but would cause more problems later on."

"I know what you mean, Jeff," answered Julie. "Let's look at this material Dr. Howard gave us and see if it answers any of our questions."

One of the most difficult decisions you will face as the parent of an ADHD child, is whether to use medication. If your child has an infection, you may give an antibiotic for a few days, and the problem is resolved. In contrast, the drugs given to manage ADHD must be taken for months and sometimes years. You can't help but wonder how this long-term usage might affect your child. The following discussion will attempt to answer the most common concerns parents have about medication for attention deficit.

Psychostimulant Medication

Psychostimulant medication is the most common treatment for children with ADHD. More children receive medication to manage ADHD than for any other childhood disorder. More research has been conducted on the effects of stimulant medications on the functioning of children with ADHD than for any other treatment modality for any childhood disorder. This extensive research helps us be fairly definitive about the benefits and liabilities of medication.

In general, we can say that medication intervention is a significant help to ADHD children.[1,2] Yet, it is true that there are all too frequent occasions when medications are improperly prescribed and monitored. If medication is to be considered, it must follow strict controls, appropriate dosages, and careful monitoring.

The most important concept to emerge from the vast amounts of research about ADHD is that no treatment approach is successful alone. Neither medical, behavioral, psychological, nor educational intervention is adequate by itself. We must be conscious of treating the *whole* child or adolescent. Successful intervention makes a difference both on the short term and on the long term. We want to make changes which will help bring about the necessary confidence, competence, organization, discipline, and character in your child. But we also want changes that will last a lifetime. The teacher may complain that your child won't sit still in the classroom. You may be unhappy that he can't remember directions. We must deal with those immediate concerns, as well as looking to his future needs. Giving the child 10 mg of

Ritalin® may help him sit in his seat and remember directions. However, it will not help him make friends.

Research has shown that multidisciplinary approaches to the treatment of ADHD work better, in the long term, than medication alone. Possibly one of the greatest benefits of stimulant therapy is that it maximizes the effects of concurrently applied treatments. What we often see is that the total treatment is far more effective than any of the components taken alone. Medication will not make your child act perfect, nor will it make him smarter. But what it can do is to reduce many of his attention difficulties so that he can tackle his problems more successfully.

The history of stimulant drug use dates back to the discovery by Bradley in 1937 of the therapeutic effects of Benzedrine® on behaviorally disturbed children. In 1948 Dexadrine® was introduced with the advantage of having equal efficacy at half the dose. Ritalin® was released in 1954 with the hope it would have fewer side effects and less abuse potential. Today Ritalin® is used in over 90 percent of cases where some type of stimulant medication is prescribed.

It is thought that stimulant drugs act by affecting the catecholamine neurotransmitters (especially dopamine) in the brain. Some believe that ADHD develops from a dopamine deficiency, which can be corrected by stimulant drug treatment. At one time it was felt stimulant drugs created a paradoxical reaction in ADHD youngsters. The paradox was the calming response to taking a stimulant drug. This is no longer believed to be the case. We now have a better, although incomplete, understanding of how the calming reaction is produced in the brain.

Many parents feel guilty about having their child take medication because they mistakenly think they are tranquilizing him. This is simply not true. The medication helps stimulate the parts of the brain needed to concentrate and attend. The decrease in external movement does not mean he has been tranquilized. It means he is able to focus more effectively. When your child is watching TV or playing a video game, he may seem oblivious to the outside world. But that doesn't mean he is tranquilized by the TV; rather, his attention is temporarily focused so that he seems mesmerized.[3]

Attention deficit results from the malfunction of the attention system. This system allows the brain to discriminate between situations where focused, deliberate behavior is appropriate and situations where quick, impulsive actions are needed. ADHD children are not able to control their attentional skills. They may be intently concentrating when they should be aware of their surroundings. On the other hand, they may be too easily distracted and ready to run off when they should be focused. Medication works to enhance the functioning of the attentional system, so that children can choose when to be sensitive to outside distractions and when to focus their attention. The attention center is stimulated by these medications with the result that the child has better control.[4]

The decision to proceed with medication intervention must be based on the comparison of the risks, benefits, and alternative treatments available. We will look at these considerations one at a time.

Short-Term Side Effects

After reviewing 110 studies, including more than 4,200 hyperactive children, one researcher concluded that the primary side effects noted for stimulants were insomnia, anorexia or loss of appetite, weight loss, and irritability. These and other side effects were reported to be transitory and to disappear with a reduction in drug dosage.[5, 6, 7]

Most of these side effects appear at the beginning of treatment. For example, your child may say to you, "My stomach doesn't feel good." Usually this feeling is not nausea, although young children may locate the sick feeling in their stomach. These complaints normally last for about a week and may not be affected by whether the child takes the medication before or after meals.

Appetite suppression is common. Your child may be less hungry for a time. This may be less noticeable if the drugs are taken after meals, since the effects wear off before the next meal. Adjusting the dosage can usually alleviate this symptom over a week or two. Since the effects of Ritalin®

last for only three to four hours, the dosage around meal-times can usually be adjusted to avoid any serious problems with appetite. Make sure your child eats a good breakfast and dinner, and supplement with nutritious after-school and bed-time snacks. This helps avoid any temporary weight loss.[8]

Other mild, but less common, side effects can include sad-ness, depression, fearfulness, social withdrawal, sleepiness, headaches, nail biting, and stomach upset. These symptoms will usually resolve spontaneously with a decrease in dosage. For example, if a child gets a headache right after taking the medicine, he may be taking too high a dose. Late-in-the-day headaches can also occur. These should be monitored closely. If they persist or are severe, the doctor will need to adjust the dosage. Some of these symptoms can be considered ac-ceptable side effects in light of clinical improvement. The parents and physician will need to make the decision regard-ing the advantages of decreased distractibility versus side effects such as nail biting. These side effects are mild, but they can occur in some children treated with stimulant medication.[5]

Toxic psychosis and seizures have occurred in a very few cases. The symptoms resolved when the medication was dis-continued. Children with a family history of epilepsy may be at greater risk, and the physician should consider this when evaluating the possibility of stimulant medication treatment.

One side effect is the possibility of nervous tics produced by stimulant medications. A number of irreversible instances of Tourette's disorder have also been reported as a result of stimulant treatment. Tourette's disorder is a neurological condition composed of multiple, persistent motor tics and uncontrolled language. The combination of motor and vocal tics is considered an important diagnostic sign although they need not be occurring at the same point in time. It is essen-tial that a child who shows signs of tics be carefully evaluated by an expert before ever taking any medication.

Perhaps fewer than 1 percent of ADHD children treated with stimulants will develop a tic disorder. Also, in 13 percent of the cases, stimulants may exacerbate preexisting tics. Therefore, it is prudent to screen children with ADHD for a personal or family history of tics or Tourette's disorder prior to initiating stimulant therapy.

Another side effect that has been reported is a "behavioral rebound" phenomenon. Typically, this is described as a deterioration in behavior that occurs in the late afternoon and evening following daytime administrations of medication. What parents report is that the child becomes very moody and irritable for the first hour or two after the medication has worn off. Research has suggested that this usually happens only for the first two or three weeks that the child is on the medication. If the problem continues or is severe, adjustments in the medication dosage and scheduling should resolve the problem.

The general consensus is that stimulant medication is relatively safe, but side effects do occur. But in the vast majority of cases, either the side effects cease after one or two weeks of continued treatment, or adjustment in the dosage alleviates the problem. You can protect your child by making sure both you and your doctor are closely monitoring side effects as well as effectiveness. Most of the serious side effects show up right away. They will also disappear quickly if the drug is withdrawn. Then a trial of a different stimulant medication can be initiated.

Long-Term Side Effects

There are no reported cases of addiction or serious drug dependence with these medications. Studies have examined the question of whether children on these drugs are more likely to abuse other substances as teenagers, compared to children not taking stimulant medications. The results suggest there is no increase in the likelihood of drug abuse.[9] In fact some youngsters adopt a stand of staunch opposition to any drugs. More research is needed on this topic since all of the issues are not yet clear. But the risk of future drug abuse appears to be quite low.

Since ADHD is a long-term condition, medical treatment may be required for a prolonged period. This also raises the question of whether the child will become tolerant of the medication. The answer appears to be no. Over time, the child's dosages may need to be increased. But this probably relates more to their increase in body weight than to their becoming tolerant of a certain dose, although it is possible for a few children to become tolerant of Ritalin®. You and your doctor should continue to monitor its effectiveness very closely.[10]

Another possible long-term side effect is the suppression of height and weight gain. Presently, it is believed that suppression in growth is a relatively transient side effect in the first year or so of treatment, and has no significant effect on eventual adult height and weight. Furthermore, there is evidence to suggest that if medication is discontinued at various points in the year, a growth rebound will occur. Most physicians will suggest a "drug holiday" especially for all or part of the summer to provide a catch-up period. One flaw in this idea is that children often have growth spurts in the summer, regardless of whether they are on medication or not. If you take your child off of the medication and he grows an inch or two, you might assume that this drug holiday caused the growth spurt. Yet, it might have happened anyway, because this is the time when most surges in height and weight take place.

Meanwhile, the summer may have been anything but a vacation. If there was a resumption of the overactivity, impulsiveness, and distractibility, you need to evaluate the relative value of stopping the medication. Ultimately, these children will reach their projected adult height. Still, it is wise for the physician to monitor growth in children receiving stimulant medications.[2]

About the time they hit adolescence, a number of children who had cooperated previously become resistant to taking their medication. Parents begin to find pills fertilizing the ferns in the family room. If they are unaware of the noncompliance, parents might assume the medication is losing its effectiveness. In reality, the child has outgrown his willingness to take the medication.

Teens don't want to be different. Taking medication separates them from the crowd. Even time-released pills taken in the privacy of their own room may not overcome the resistance. Open discussion, careful supervision, and understanding of your child's feelings can help him work through this opposition.

Contraindications: Reasons for Avoiding or Stopping Medication

With what we now know about stimulant medication, *contraindications* include: known hypersensitivity or allergic reaction to the drug; seizure history; glaucoma; hypertension; history of tics; hyperthyroidism; and pregnancy. One of the main objectives of the physical exam is to determine whether your child fits any of the predisposing categories. Liver disease, certain forms of heart disease, and high blood pressure are the clearest contraindications to stimulant therapy. Children with seizure disorders should probably not take stimulants, since the drug can lower the seizure threshold and increase the likelihood of seizures.

Doctors are also reluctant to use stimulants in children with a family history of tics, because stimulants can increase the possibility of tics developing. Stimulants can also aggravate anxiety. If a child who has ADHD is also quite anxious, an alternative to stimulant medication may be appropriate.

Most physicians will be reluctant to prescribe medication for a preschool child. Only if there are extreme symptoms, and if the child is a danger to himself, would stimulant medication be appropriate.[8] The use of behavioral management techniques is a preferred method of treatment.

Benefits of Medication

Between 70 and 80 percent of children appear to exhibit a positive response to stimulant medication. There seems to be three general categories of response to medication.

For about 20 to 30 percent of the children, medication brings about a dramatic improvement. This would be the *"Praise the Lord—it's a miracle!"* category. The effect is both immediate and obvious. Often within the first hour after treatment a perceptible change in handwriting, talking, motility, attending, organization, and perception may be observed. Classroom teachers may notice improvement in deportment and academic productivity after a single dose. Off-task activity levels seem to decrease and the child becomes more compliant and less aggressive. Parents will report a marked reduction in troublesome sibling interactions, inappropriate activity, and noncompliance. Even peers can identify the calmer, more organizing, cooperative behavior of stimulant-treated children.[11]

The next general category of response is, *"Well, I guess it helps."* While parents and teachers notice improvement in the child's attention and self-control, the effects are not astonishing. The child is definitely easier to teach because he's not quite so fidgety and distractible, but he still requires a ton of extra attention. Most children will fall into this category. There are significant improvements, but not wholesale changes.

The last category of medication response is, *"This stuff is no good!"* Some children either don't respond or react poorly to medication. Despite all efforts to find the right medication at the right dose, a positive reaction is not obtained. In other cases, there is some positive effect on attention and self-control, but the side effects make the improvements "not worth it."[12] It has been estimated that 1 to 3 percent of children with ADHD cannot tolerate any dose of stimulant medication.[2, 13]

In summary, the primary benefits are the improvement of the core problems of ADHD—hyperactivity, impulsivity, and inattentiveness. Attention span seems to improve and there is a reduction of disruptive, inappropriate, and impulsive behavior. Compliance with the commands of authority figures is increased, and children's peer relations may also improve, primarily through reduction in aggression. In addition, if the dosage is carefully monitored and adjusted, the medication has been found to enhance academic performance.[2]

Medication does little to rectify any cognitive functioning or learning disabilities. If a child has visual or auditory processing deficits, medication will probably not change this learning problem. What it may do is help him pay attention better, so that remedial instruction will have more of a chance to impact the learning disability.

Although these medications are certainly helpful in the day-to-day management of ADHD, they have not been demonstrated to lead to enduring positive changes after their cessation. Research has been very clear that stimulant medications are not a panacea for ADHD, and should not be the sole treatment employed in most cases. The numerous skill deficits which these children have will still need attention and remediation.

It would be a mistake to assume that because a child responds to medication he must be ADHD. Likewise, it is an error to say a child is not ADHD, if he fails to respond to medication. This says nothing about his condition. It certainly does not indicate that his problems are any less real than those who do respond. The key is a thorough evaluation that identifies all of the child's needs, followed by a detailed treatment plan. Medication may be one component of that plan.

When to Use Medication

One of the most difficult decisions for both the parent and clinician is deciding when to use medication. The fact your child has been diagnosed as ADHD does not imply an automatic recommendation for drug treatment. One author has summarized the following rules as aids in making the medication decision. I have found these guidelines to be accurate and helpful in my recommendations to parents. I suggest you talk them over with your own practitioner.

Guidelines for Recommending Medication

1. Has the child had adequate physical and psychological evaluations? Medications should never be prescribed if the child has not been recently examined in a thorough manner.

2. How old is the child? Pharmacotherapy is often less effective or leads to more severe side effects among children below the age of four and is therefore not usually recommended in such cases.

3. Have other therapies been used? If this is your first contact with a professional, prescription of medication should perhaps be postponed until other interventions have been attempted. Alternatively, when the child's behavior presents

a severe problem and the family cannot participate in child-management training, medication may be the most practical initial treatment.

4. How severe is the child's current misbehavior? In some cases, the child's behavior is so unmanageable or distressing to the family that medication may prove the fastest and most effective manner of dealing with the crisis until other forms of treatment can commence. Once progress is obtained with other therapies, some effort can be made to reduce or terminate the medication. This is not always possible.

5. Can you as a family afford the medication and associated costs? Long-term compliance is very important. You need to be willing and able to stick with the treatment program as long as your clinician recommends it.

6. Do you feel able to supervise and monitor the use of the medications and guard against their abuse? If your own life is too disorganized and stressful, you may not be able to see that your child maintains the proper medication schedule.

7. What is your attitude toward medication? Some parents are simply anti-drug and should not be coerced into agreeing to this treatment. If you really don't want your child on medication, your underlying attitude will probably sabotage its efficacy.

8. Is there a delinquent sibling or drug-abusing parent in the household? If so, psychostimulant medication should not be prescribed, since there is a high risk of its illicit use or sale.

9. Does your child have any history of tics, psychosis, or thought disorder? If so, the stimulants are contraindicated, as they may exacerbate such difficulties.

10. Is your child highly anxious, fearful, or likely to complain of psychosomatic disturbances? Such a child is less likely to respond positively to stimulant medications and may exhibit a better response to antidepressant medications.

11. Does your physician have the time to monitor medication effects properly? In addition to an initial assessment of drug efficacy and establishment of the optimal dosage, periodic reassessment of drug response and effects on height and

weight should be conducted throughout the year.

12. How does your child feel about medication and its alternatives? With older children and adolescents, it is important that the use of medication be discussed with them and its rationale fully explained. In cases where children are anti-drug or oppositional, they may sabotage efforts to use it. Sometimes the "wearing glasses for a visual handicap" metaphor can help explain medication without a stigma.[2]

Prescribing Procedures

Ritalin® (methylphenidate) is available in 5, 10, and 20 mg tablets. This is a short-acting tablet which most commonly lasts four hours. Ritalin-SR® is a sustained-release product with effects lasting six to eight hours. Some physicians report unsatisfactory reliability with the sustained-release form of Ritalin®.[14, 12] The usual dosage is .3 milligrams per kilogram (about 2.2 pounds) of body weight up to 1 milligram per kilogram in a 24-hour period. The usual starting dosage of the standard Ritalin® for children under eight is a single 5 mg tablet in the morning, and for children over eight a single 10 mg tablet in the morning. Each week the daily dosage can be increased by 5 mg and 10 mg a day, respectively. Usually tablets are taken at breakfast and lunch. Occasionally an after-school dose is necessary. The total maximum daily dosage should not exceed 60 mg, although under extreme situations 80 mg/day dosages are prescribed.[1]

The amphetamines are quite similar in their pharmacologic makeup. Dexedrine® (d-amphetamine) comes in 5, 10, and 15 mg tablets and capsules; in a liquid elixir preparation with 5 mg per teaspoon; and in slow-release capsules of 5, 10, and 15 mg. The dosage is approximately half that of Ritalin®.

Benzedrine® is available in 5, 10, and 15 mg tablets; and in a 15 mg sustained-release capsule. The dosage range is similar to Dexedrine® (5-60 mg/day).

Desoxyn® is available in 2.5 and 5 mg tablets; and in 5, 10, and 15 mg sustained-release capsules. Pharmacological actions are similar to those of Dexedrine and Benzedrine.

Cylert® (pemoline) is taken once a day, giving it an advantage over the shorter-acting preparations. It has a gradual onset of action. Significant clinical benefits may not be evident until the third or fourth week of treatment, and they may take as long as six weeks. The drug is available in 18.75, 37.5, and 75 mg tablets; and in 37.5 mg chewable tablets. The recommended starting dose is 37.5 mg and the dosage is increased in daily increments of 18.75 mg per week until the desired clinical effects are reached. The effective daily dose for most patients is in the range between 56.25–75 mg. The maximum daily dose is 112.5 mg. Periodic liver function tests are required.[1]

Tricyclic antidepressants including Tofranil® (imipramine) and Norpramine® (desiprimine) have also been prescribed for the treatment of ADHD. The bulk of the research suggests that overall, psychostimulants tend to be superior to the tricyclics in managing ADHD symptoms. However, there may be a subgroup of children, particularly those who show signs of anxiety, depression, sleep problems, or who have tics or psychosis, who may respond better to the tricyclics.

Clonidine® (catapres) is an antihypertensive medication that has recently been used to treat ADHD symptoms. Its frequency of side effects in ADHD children has not yet clearly been demonstrated. It is available in transdermal skin patches which allows the release of medicine evenly all day. Since Clonidine® is also used for treatment of Tourette's syndrome, it may prove useful in ADHD children who have tics or who have developed tics on methylphenidate.

Prozac® (fluoxetine), the nation's most prescribed antidepressant, has recently been used with ADHD children. However, at this time there is very little research to document its usefulness with ADHD children.

No matter which medication is employed, some common principles should apply. I have summarized the major ideas proposed by various authors in regard to the use of medication with ADHD children.

Prescription Principles

1. The dose should be the lowest possible and be given only as many times per day as necessary to achieve adequate management of the child's behavior.

2. In most cases medication should be discontinued on holidays or summer vacations, unless absolutely necessary.

3. Titration (dosage) should be based on objective assessment of the child's resulting behavior and should start with the lowest possible increments.

4. Sufficient time (5 to 7 days) should be allowed for evaluation of the efficacy of each dosage.

5. Parents should never be given permission to adjust the dosage of medication without consultation with the physician. This often leads to overmedication of a child, since the parents may increase the dosage every time the child misbehaves.[2]

6. Never force medication on a child or family, particularly adolescents.

7. The physician should provide accurate information to the family about all aspects of the medication.

Evaluation of Medical Intervention

The response of each child to medication is different. Therefore, it is important to collect objective data regarding changes in your child's behavior across several doses. The best approach is to determine the child's optimal dose in the context of a double-blind, placebo-controlled assessment study that includes multiple measures of the child's behavior collected from the home, school, and clinic. Double-blind means neither the physician nor parent knows when your child is receiving the stimulant medication and when he is taking a neutral substance called a placebo. The use of a placebo reduces the effects of positive biases that can show up on rating scales when the rater knows the child is taking a medication.

This type of process usually takes three weeks. During one of those weeks the child is on a small dosage of Ritalin®, such as 5 mg. A 10 mg dosage is used during another week, and the placebo occupies the third week. The sequence is known only to the nurse, technician, or pharmacist who prepares or dispenses the prescriptions.

It is also important during this time not to make any drastic changes in school or intervention techniques. To do so would contaminate the effects of the medication. Later on, several different treatment strategies will be used for your child. But for the time the medication study is taking place, don't make other changes.

At the end of each week, both the parents and teacher complete a rating scale of some type. This is done to objectively measure the child's behavior during that particular week. The types of measures used to make the original diagnosis of ADHD now offer a comparison point for your child's performances on medication. The initial standardized score your child received allowed the clinician to compare him to other children. Now, the weekly scores provided by the parent and teacher allow him to be compared to himself. If there are any improvements in behavior that correspond to the introduction of the various medications, your doctor can assume the changes are primarily due to the medication. If one level of dosage was also accompanied by the most significant improvements in behavior, that level may become the initial therapeutic dosage. Periodic measurements are necessary to evaluate the continued efficacy of the treatment.

Whether or not your physician uses a double-blind study, some type of objective measures are needed. The *Revised Conner's Teacher and Parent Rating Scales (CPRS/CTRS)*, the ADD *Comprehensive Teacher Rating Scale (ACTeRs)*, the *Home Situations Questionnaire (HSQ)*, and the *School Situations Questionnaire (SSQ)* are often used for this purpose. These were all described in chapter 3. Their purpose is to make sure the medication is actually helping your child. If the data and your observations don't support any improvement, then the medication must be adjusted or dropped. Sometimes it takes a month or two to settle on a medication program that suits your child. Be patient. Don't drop the whole idea because there are no significant improvements in the first week. Also keep in mind the short-acting nature of Ritalin® and Dexedrine®. When you see your child in the evening, the effects may have worn off. But the teacher may still see positive changes during the day. Make sure you look at all aspects of your child's day before you decide to stop the medication.

What to Tell Your Child?

If medication is eventually prescribed, it is important to be honest with your child. Don't call it a vitamin or an allergy pill. Explain that the medication will make it easier to concentrate, complete his assignments, and get along with his friends. Your child needs to be told that medication will not solve all of his problems. It will not make him smarter—he is smart enough already. However, it will make it easier to pay attention to his teacher and schoolwork. A child can be told, "If you work very hard, you will probably finish your assignments and do better in school." The key idea is *hard work*.

Your child needs to be responsible for his own actions. Don't let him use forgotten or worn-off medication as an excuse for inappropriate actions or failure to complete homework. Also, refrain from making comments that link a child's undesirable behaviors to a need for medication. Avoid saying, "You're acting like you need another pill," or "You wouldn't have gotten in trouble today if you'd taken your medicine at lunch." The medication should not be seen as an all-controlling force outside the child. Medication can be beneficial, but the child must know that he is still in control of his actions. He alone is responsible for his academic and social accomplishments. On the other side of the coin, he is ultimately responsible for his mistakes.

The choice to use medication is important. The decision does not end when you start your child on a medication. Careful monitoring must be done to evaluate the effects and to determine the proper dosage. Side effects are possible, so careful observation of your child is necessary. Keep in contact with your physician.

Remember, medication is never the sole treatment program. What you do *after* the start of medication is where the major benefits accrue. The effects of medication alone are temporary. The effects of instruction and self-control will last a lifetime. Medication is one aspect of a balanced treatment.

Other Medical Interventions

Any concurrent illnesses or conditions such as allergies should be treated as effectively as possible. Research has not validated concerns about food additives, sugar, or diet. While this lack of evidence may be true for groups of children, there still may be a relationship with your particular child. I would encourage you to follow standard medical, nutritional, and psychological practice that has been demonstrated to be valid. If you wish to explore other forms of intervention, be cautious and be careful with your money. Examine the basis of the claims made for a particular treatment. Does it have only anecdotal support? Has it been submitted to scientific scrutiny? Has any professional organization taken a stand one way or the other on the particular idea you are considering?

A book by Keith Conners, *Feeding the Brain: How Foods Affect Children,* presents a balanced and fair review of the effects of diet, vitamins, additives, and environmental toxins on children's behavior and functioning. It is a good resource if you wish to follow this topic in more detail.[15] Another book by John Taylor, *Helping Your Hyperactive Child,* presents a supportive view of the Feingold diet as one of several options for treating ADHD children. He reports no real data to substantiate his positive convictions about the Feingold program, but does provide guidelines for utilizing the program.[16]

Pay attention to your child's response to various environmental influences. You can develop a good sense of how different environmental factors influence your son or daughter. Remember to alter only one thing at a time. But if you can see definite agents that cause your child's behavior to fluctuate, bring these to the attention of the appropriate professional. Don't give up. Some nontraditional approaches could have potential. However, don't commit yourself until there is evidence for trying a specific idea.

A scientific study should have most of the following characteristics or components.

• A placebo versus actual therapy trial where one group of children receives the actual treatment and another group receives treatment that appears to be similar, but omits the specific intervention being studied.

• A random assignment of subjects to each of the groups.

• Double-blind methods in which no member of the study knows who is actually being treated and who is not.

• A standard evaluation procedure where each child is followed for a specific length of time, with recognized measurement tools, so effects and side effects of treatment can be monitored.

• The use of appropriate statistical analysis, in which each study is analyzed with careful accounting methods to determine the actual success rate.

Questions about Medical Interventions

1. Is it true that stimulant medications are mind-altering drugs?

Yes, you could say stimulants such as Ritalin® do change the composition of the brain. But this is true only in terms of activating the attention, body movement, organization, motivation, and planning abilities of the brain.

Stimulant medications are definitely *not* mind-altering drugs in terms of changing one's personality or one's perceptions of reality. Although stimulant medications may help a child to better focus his attention, delay impulsive responding, and organize himself in a more efficient manner, they do not cause him to experience distortions of reality. They are no more mind-altering than aspirin, which causes a reduction of pain messages to the brain.

2. Could large doses of certain vitamins help my child?

Some health food devotees and nutritionists advocate massive ingestion of certain vitamins for a variety of problems. To the best of our knowledge, there is no evidence to support the efficacy of this for the treatment of ADHD. What studies do exist tend to support the idea that megavitamins are ineffective in reducing the symptoms of ADHD children. Of significant concern is the possibility of toxic blood levels from too high a level of vitamin intake. The supposed advantage of vitamin therapy over drug therapy, in being less toxic, thus becomes somewhat questionable.[15] Too much of anything can be dangerous.[12]

3. What about giving a child with ADHD symptoms coffee to help calm him down?

At least ten studies have shown that caffeine, whether in coffee or in a tablet, has no measurable positive impact on the inattention of an ADHD youngster. About the only thing you can count on is that your child will have to go to the bathroom more often. This can add to his avoidance behavior, since he will now spend much of the morning running to the lavatory.

References

1. Barkley, R.A., *Attention-Deficit Hyperactivity Disorder: A Clinical Workbook* (New York: The Guilford Press, 1991).

2. Barkley, R.A., *Attention-Deficit Hyperactivity Disorder. A Handbook for Diagnosis and Treatment* (New York: The Guilford Press, 1990).

3. Garber, S.W., Garber, M.D., and Spizman, R.F., *If Your Child Is Hyperactive, Inattentive, Impulsive, Distractible ... Helping the ADD Hyperactive Child* (New York: Villard Books, 1990).

4. Goldstein, S., and Goldstein, M., *Managing Attention Disorders in Children* (New York: John Wiley & Sons, 1990).

5. Ross, D.M., and Ross, S.A., *Hyperactivity: Current Issues, Research, and Theory*, 2nd ed. (New York: Wiley, 1982).

6. Barkley, R.A., "A Review of Stimulant Drug Research with Hyperactive Children," *Journal of Child Psychology and Psychiatry* 18 (1977):137–65.

7. Barkley, R.A., "Predicting the Response of Hyperkinetic Children to Stimulant Drugs: A Review," *Journal of Abnormal Child Psychology*, 4 (1976):327–48.

8. Moss, R.A., *Why Johnny Can't Concentrate: Coping with Attention-Deficit Problems* (New York: Bantam Books, 1990).

9. Gadow, K.D., "Prevalence of Drug Treatment for Hyperactivity and Other Childhood Behavior Disorders," *Psychosocial Aspects of Drug Treatment for Hyperactivity*, ed. Gadow,

K.D., and Loney, J. (Boulder, Colorado: Westview Press, 1981), 13–70.

10. Bain, L.J., *Attention Deficit Disorders* (New York: Dell Publishing, 1991).

11. Conners, C.K., and Wells, K.C., *Hyperkinetic Children: A Neuropsychological Approach* (Beverly Hills, California: Sage, 1986).

12. Gordon, M., *ADHD/Hyperactivity: A Consumer's Guide* (DeWitt, New York: GSI Publications, 1991).

13. Barkley, R.A., "Tic Disorders and Tourette's Syndrome," *Behavioral Assessment of Childhood Disorders,* ed. Marsh, E., and Terdal, L. 2nd ed. (New York: The Guilford Press, 1988). 69–104.

14. Goldstein, S., and Goldstein, M., "The Multi-Disciplinary Evaluation and Treatment of Children with Attention-Deficit Disorders," 16th ed. (Salt Lake City: Neurology, Learning and Behavior Center, 1991).

15. Conners, C.K., *Feeding the Brain: How Foods Affect Children* (New York: Plenum Press, 1989).

16. Taylor, J.F., *Helping Your Hyperactive Child* (Rocklin, California: Prima Publishing & Communications, 1990).

ChAPTER SeVEN

HOW CAN THE SCHOOL HELP?
Educational Issues in ADHD Treatment

It's no wonder an ADHD child has problems with school. Nowhere else is he required to concentrate so long in the face of so many powerful distractions. Successful performance in school is dependent on an ability to persist and maintain concentration for long periods of time. All students must learn class routines, conform to teacher's rules, and inhibit their impulses to do otherwise. Furthermore, the student must control his body movement, maintain an appropriate level of arousal, and delay gratification until report cards are issued.

If you were to set out to design a situation that was most *contrary* to the needs and abilities of an ADHD student, you would probably come up with a typical classroom. We ask a child who has profound problems attending, organizing, and controlling his actions to spend hours per day attending, organizing, and controlling his actions. Would we ask a hearing-impaired child to listen to lectures all day, or a vision-impaired child to watch movies, and then hold them accountable for the content? I think not. But, in essence, this is what we ask of an ADHD child.

Our educational system is demanding more of these skills, and at an earlier age. As a result the ADHD child will experience increased frustration and failure. Because of the child's problems, it is often the classroom teacher who raises questions that bring about referrals for an evaluation. While the teacher knows your child has a problem, confusion may arise over what *kind* of problem it is and what to *do* about it. Unless the teacher believes your child's diagnosis of ADHD is well-founded and real, it may be hard for you to convince him or her to make all the necessary modifications for your child.

Some teachers bristle at the idea of making adjustments. "Why should I give him more time to complete his assignment or cut his assignment in half? He's smart enough to do the work if he'd only buckle down and do it. Your child has an attitude problem, not an attention problem." The prevailing opinion among unconvinced teachers is that ADHD children are just irresponsible, lazy, immature, or spoiled. One of your first jobs, as an advocate for your child, is to help school personnel appreciate the legitimacy of the ADHD diagnosis. They also must become familiar with the essential characteristics of the problem. This might require you to provide written materials, recommend workshops, identify videos, and organize training meetings to help bring the school personnel up to speed on the requirements of the ADHD student. The mental health professional who has worked with you so far should be a good resource for working with the school.

Appropriate Education for Teachers

I will highlight some general ideas for communicating the nature and needs of an ADHD student to his classroom teacher.

● The teacher must be *educated* about the cause and nature of attention disorders, and understand the developmental perspective of the attention-related impairment. It is necessary for the teacher to make the same distinction as the parents do between noncompliance and incompetence. The differential effects of various consequences must be understood. An ADHD student may not respond to the same arrangement of rewards and punishments as do other students. How this impacts classroom management must be conveyed to the teacher in practical and nonthreatening ways.

• The next step in the process is to *pinpoint* the most problematic areas of concern. Because an ADHD child can have so many inappropriate classroom behaviors, it is necessary to identify and define those that need immediate attention. This is much like a triage decision in emergency medicine and many problems exist. Your child has numerous educational needs, but you can't work with all of those needs at once. Problems must be prioritized and specific intervention procedures developed for each area of concern. Usually, there will be two types of intervention. There are self-management procedures aimed at helping the child take control of his own behavior. There are also interventions which alter the school environment in order to help the child function more effectively. I will give examples of these interventions a little later in this chapter.

• Teachers can be educated about the *definition, cause,* and *developmental nature of attention disorders* through books, pamphlets, videos, workshops, and personal communication. Schools often provide such training resources. However, as an advocate for your child, you can become aware of some short texts and pamphlets written especially for teachers.

The Neurology, Learning & Behavior Center has both a booklet, *Teacher's Guide: Attention-Deficit Hyperactive Disorders in Children,* and a two-hour training video, *Educating Inattentive Children,* that are very useful.

Other video resources include: *Understanding Attention Deficit Disorders (ADD),* by Copeland (3 C's of Childhood, Inc., 1989) and *All About Attention Deficit Disorder,* by Phelan (Child Management, 1989).

The *ADD Hyperactivity Workbook for Parents, Teachers and Kids* by Parker (Impact, 1988), *Attention Without Tension: A Teacher's Handbook on Attention Disorders (ADHD/ADD)* by Copeland and Love (3 C's of Childhood, Inc., 1990), and the

Attention Deficit Disorders Intervention Manual: School Version, by McCarney (Hawthorne, 1989) are appropriate references which include intervention ideas. All of these materials can be obtained by mail through A.D.D. WareHouse; the address is given in Part Three.

Obtaining Help from the School

● *Legislative mandate.* For a number of years, ADHD students could qualify for special education services under Public Law 94-142 only if they had other problems such as learning disabilities or emotional disturbances. This has caused parent groups to become very active in encouraging Congress to allow ADHD to qualify for services.

In the fall of 1991, the U.S. Education Department sent a letter to state school superintendents advising them of their responsibility to service ADHD students.[1] The letter outlined three ways students with ADHD could receive assistance through special education programs.

The first method of eligibility has been available for some time. Students diagnosed with ADHD *in addition* to other disabilities, such as emotional disturbances or learning disabilities, may receive federally funded special education by virtue of those other diagnoses. This represents no change.

Children who have only ADHD, but whose alertness is chronically or acutely impaired by the disorder, may now receive services under the category of *"other health impaired."* Previous to this letter, there was confusion over whether this catchall category applied to ADHD children. As of this writing, it does apply.

The third way students may qualify is under Section 504 of the Rehabilitation Act of 1973. Schools do not receive any federal funding for students classified under Section 504. However, the law does obligate schools to modify classroom practices for any students whose physical or mental impairments substantially limit their learning ability. This section of the Education Department letter encourages interventions for the regular classroom. The examples of adaptations in regular education programs mentioned in the Department of Education letter include:

Providing a structured learning environment; repeating and simplifying instructions about in-class and home-work assignments; supplementing verbal instructions with visual instructions; using behavioral management techniques; adjusting class schedules; modifying test de-livery; using tape recorders, computer-aided instruction, and other audiovisual equipment; selecting modified textbooks or workbooks; and tailoring homework as-signments.[1]

There is still mixed opinion about providing services to ADHD children. The guidelines are likely to change, so you are advised to keep abreast of the developments within your local school district. What this means, though, is that the chances are better now for you to get help for your child, even if he "only" has ADHD.

• *Obtaining educational services.* The specific process varies with each school district, but the following description should come pretty close to what can happen if you or the school should initiate the process. The first step is for a parent or teacher to make a referral. In my state it is called a "focus of concern." This means you fill out a form available from your child's school that identifies learning problems which impact your child's educational program. This referral is processed through the school principal and goes to the district pupil services department. A child study team is formed to act on the referral. Usually this team consists of a school psycholo-gist or counselor, nurse, and educational specialist, along with your child's teacher and principal. The school district is obli-gated to process your referral within 45–90 days, obtain initial information about your child, and make a recommendation for services. During this time various members of the team will review the child's school folder, talk to the teacher, observe him in the classroom, obtain various rating scales, and possi-bly complete individual testing.

You will be notified of what is transpiring and probably will be given various forms to complete, including background information and descriptions of the current problem. A "focus of concern" child study is supposed to include the emotional, social, and physical dimensions of a child, as well as the educational. So you may be asked to have your child seen by your physician, who will then send a report back to the child study team. If the school district does not have a specialist available to evaluate a specific part of the referring question, they may refer to an appropriate professional such as a psychologist. Generally, when the school makes this type of referral, they are obligated to pay for it. Make sure that is clear in your case.

After the study team has gathered all of the data and observations about your child, you will be invited to a meeting to discuss the findings and recommendations and to agree upon some type of Individual Educational Plan (IEP). In the case of ADHD, you might agree to modifications in the classroom management and assignment reductions. Medication may or may not be recommended. All of this would be discussed at that meeting. In complicated cases, several such meetings would be held over the school year.

The school can address only educational concerns. That is appropriate and significant. Your child spends about five hours of each day in the school environment. ADHD children need a total program of intervention. So even if the study team recommends adjustments to the classroom, you will still need help and advice about how to make changes at home. Thus, an outside resource will often still be necessary, unless the district has the appropriate personnel to assign to you.

Even if you do not utilize the resources of your local school district at the beginning, your child's teacher will still be a vital part of the treatment plan. As I said in chapter 3, part of choosing an outside professional is to select someone who is skilled and able to work closely with the school. This means that your child's teacher is a crucial part of the intervention process.

To penetrate the ADHD child's "thick barrier," his world has to provide him with unusual amounts of structure and flexibility. Often the regular classroom is limited in the extent to which these needs can be met. The classroom places a premium on self-control and sustained attention. At the same time, consequences for failure to conform tend to be inconsistent, infrequent, and delayed. An ADHD child is drawn to events that are most stimulating and intriguing. Unfortunately, this usually means it is more fun to watch a fly on the ceiling or to pass notes to a classmate than to complete a sheet of long division.

An ADHD child will impulsively grab for attention wherever and whenever it may come his way. In most classrooms this means he will get attention for doing something wrong more often than for doing something right. Such limitations of the learning environment strongly suggest that there is need for change in the classroom, if an ADHD child is going to have a better chance of survival and success.

Dr. Michael Gordon has summarized the essential needs of an ADHD child. I believe this list gives us a good overview of where we need to head in terms of changes for your child. Keep these needs in mind as you work with the school to develop programs for your child.

Essential Classroom Needs of an ADHD Child[2]

1. Clearly specified rules, expectations, and instructions.
2. Frequent, immediate, and consistent feedback on behavior, and redirection to task.
3. Reasonable and meaningful consequences for both compliance and noncompliance.
4. Programming and adult intervention designed to compensate for the child's distractibility, limited organizational skills, and low frustration tolerance.
5. A well-integrated and functioning team of parents, teachers, administrators, and clinician who communicate often and work together to create a structured and supportive environment.

• *Strategies for classroom assistance.* Most schools will take a three-step approach to providing educational services to a child.

Step one provides modifications within the regular classroom. This usually entails consulting with the teacher, making sure he or she is knowledgeable about ADHD and implementing classroom management programs tailored for the mainstreamed setting.

Keeping students in the regular classroom, or mainstreaming, is the presumption of most schools. The most desirable alternative is to help the ADHD child function successfully in the regular classroom. This "least restrictive environment" principle directs schools to establish programs that allow handicapped children to interact with nonhandicapped peers as much as possible. Most school districts will err in the direction of not segregating special needs children. Of course, this is also the least expensive option.

Step two offers more intensive services through a combination of regular and resource room activities. This may entail the child leaving class for an hour or more per day in order to receive individual attention. Sometimes the resource room teacher will come into the child's class and work with him there. Additional services are added as needed for situations where the child might require special help, such as language or learning deficiencies.

Step three involves special class placement for most of the child's school day. This is required when the ADHD child has significant emotional, behavioral, or learning problems.

ADHD children require help at least at the first step and often at the second step of assistance. Often the focus of the resource room activity can be on review and organization of regular classroom assignments. This is in contrast to trying to instruct the student in skills using tasks unrelated to current classroom assignments. Frequently, ADHD children need to sit down on a one-to-one basis and go over the assignments they had trouble focusing on in class. This can be a time to make sure that all the homework assignments are understood and recorded prior to taking work home. The resource room teacher can also be a primary liaison between the school and parent, helping coordinate incentive efforts, providing daily report cards, and facilitating feedback. Of course, the resource teacher can also provide remedial help in basic skills.

There is no definite bench mark for moving from one level of intervention to the next. It boils down to the broad question of, "Is your child making satisfactory progress under the current instructional methods?" If he is not, then more resources may be needed. Here is a simple checklist to help you look at your child's educational status.

Educational Status Checklist

Yes No

☐ ☐   1. Is your child making satisfactory academic progress? Are his progress reports and report cards satisfactory, given his potential and ability?

☐ ☐   2. Is your child's behavior maintaining at an appropriate level? (If he is being disciplined frequently, excluded from class, or spending lots of time in the principal's office, there is a problem.)

☐ ☐   3. Does your child's teacher seem generally optimistic about your child and his progress?

☐ ☐   4. Does the teacher believe s/he is able to give your child the attention he needs?

☐ ☐   5. Is your child relatively free from being a scapegoat or marked child by either the teacher or his peers?

☐ ☐   6. Does your child seem pleased and happy with school?

☐ ☐   7. Are you relatively satisfied with the school program for your child?

The more "yes" responses you have, the more likely the school program is currently meeting your child's needs. If the majority of these questions are answered in the positive, there is probably no need to pursue additional services at another level. There may always be adjustments to a treatment program, such as more time in the resource room to work on a particular problem. Maybe the student is having a harder time with long division and needs some extra help. This is the type of change that needs to be monitored closely. You don't want your child to struggle for two months in math and then get a poor report card, before you hear about it for the first time. Don't be lulled into apathy out of fatigue or by the fact you haven't heard from the school for a few weeks. I know it's tempting to believe that no news is good news. You may have spent so much time working to resolve various problems with your child that you can't bear another teacher conference. Your weariness is understandable. Yet, life with an ADHD child requires vigilance and never-ending monitoring.

Choosing the Best School

● *Public versus private schools.* Making the decision about whether to send your child to a public versus a Christian or other private school can be very difficult. Usually the private school will offer smaller class size, greater structure, and more individualized attention. For the Christian parent, the value system and spiritual content of a parochial school can be a very important consideration. The thing you need to weigh very carefully is whether the private school has the appropriate understanding of the needs of an ADHD student and is willing to make the necessary adjustments. Smaller class size is helpful, but it is not a sufficient adjustment to meet the needs of most ADHD children.

Be sure that the private school can provide both the curriculum and classroom management techniques described in this chapter. Just because a school is Christian doesn't mean it can meet the requirements of a special needs student. In fact, if I had to generalize, I would say that most Christian schools do not have the resources for special service students that most public schools can provide. This is usually a matter of economics. Most private schools struggle to maintain a balance between reasonable tuition and quality programming for their regular students. The cost of adding resource teachers and other specialists is generally beyond their reach. However, there are some notable exceptions. If these noteworthy programs exist in your area, by all means consider them as options for your child.

Another caution is in regard to a highly competitive, college preparatory curriculum. Many ADHD children are bright enough to handle this kind of program, if their attention skills are under control. Should you consider a competitive school environment for your child, make sure he or she is fully able to handle it. Generally speaking, I would say this kind of program should be avoided for most ADHD students. Consult with the clinician who completed the evaluation for an opinion on the most appropriate options for your child.

• *Home schooling.* Home schooling is an educational option that thousands of families across the country have chosen for their children. If you have the necessary time, patience, and ability, home schooling may be an appropriate option. What you need to consider is whether the demands of being both parent and teacher of an ADHD child are within your emotional capabilities. The stress of parenting is sufficient for the majority of families. However, if you are unhappy with the public and private school alternatives in your area, and you can make the additional adjustments to add instruction to your load, home schooling may work for you and your child.

Home school families usually place most of the responsibility for instruction on the mother. This is because the father is the primary source of income and is away at work most of the day. If you choose to home school, involve both parents in the instruction of your child as much as possible. This places less of a total burden on the mom and enriches the quality of experiences gained by your child.

There are many things to consider in home schooling. You will need to think about the type of textbooks or curriculum you use, fostering social experiences, measuring student progress, and meeting state guidelines. The basic approach to classroom management will still be the same as presented in the following sections.

Many areas have home school associations that band together for enrichment and training activities. For more information you can check with the National Center for Home Education at P.O. Box 125, Paeonoan Springs, VA 22129, or with the Moore Foundation, P.O. Box 1, Camas, WA 98607.

What If the School Is Uncooperative?

Most schools try very hard to help children with special needs. Countless teachers spend extra time and money out of their own pockets to develop materials for children in their classrooms. Many teachers will take on a strong advocacy role for a particular child when they believe supplementary services are necessary. Unfortunately, some schools and administrators will not respond to reasonable requests for special services. It's not always an issue of money, although that is the excuse most frequently given. Sometimes it's because of a particular philosophy or belief of a principal or administrator that ADHD does not exist, or that all children should receive the same services. In meeting with school officials, I have heard other opinions bordering on insanity!

The law provides several means through which you can challenge the school's decisions regarding your child. These range from meeting with various committees that oversee special educational services to calling a due process hearing which is presided over by an impartial judge. You can learn about these remedies by contacting your state education department or by contacting your local ADD or Learning Disabilities Association. The addresses for the national organizations are given in Part Three.

The recent inclusion of ADHD in Public Law 94–142 will go a long ways in requiring schools to respond to the needs of attention deficit students. Section 504 of the Rehabilitation Act of 1973 gives you another route to follow. Your local chapter of the various support and advocacy groups offer ideas on how to draw on these laws for the benefit of your child. In reality, you have considerable legal clout, should you need it. The Legal Services Administration has an Educational Advocacy Branch which can be tapped for legal resources, if your local efforts prove fruitless. There are times when parents need to be a forceful and informed presence in the school. This might mean that you become a bit of a nuisance, or that you band together with other parents to push for needed changes.[2]

Your best bet is to remain on a cooperative basis with your school. An adversarial relationship should be avoided, if at all possible. Nobody likes to be threatened or forced to provide services when they don't want to, and the schools are no exception. You don't want to pursue formal action until you are sure that all other avenues for negotiation have been exhausted. An extensive (and costly) legal battle to win a class adjustment for your child may leave you with such a bad taste in your mouth that you wouldn't put your child back in that program for all the tea in China. You need to establish a workable balance between active cooperation with the school and energetic insistence on change.

Once again, your clinician should be of assistance in working with the school to develop a reasonable program. As I write this chapter, I see that my schedule for next week includes an Individual Education Program (IEP) meeting with a local elementary school staff. The student has ADHD as well as some educational deficits, but the principal has expressed initial disbelief about the child's diagnosis. I will be there with data in hand to argue the child's case for needing resource room assistance in addition to his regular classroom. Several of the staff have agreed with the proposed changes, based on their knowledge of the student. I hope that my presence will help in the decision-making process. At other times, a letter from me has been sufficient to move the process along.

Remember to always keep a record of your contacts with school and other officials during the course of your efforts. It takes a bit of effort, but you should keep a log of phone calls, letters written, meetings attended, promises made, and administrative no-shows. These records can be very valuable if there is ever any legal action. Make copies of all your correspondence, and don't let the originals of anything disappear into the bureaucratic paper mill.

Classroom Management of ADHD

Although you probably can't choose your child's teacher, you should think about the best kind of classroom for your child. Invariably, ADHD children perform better in a more structured setting directed by teachers who prefer defined work patterns, rather than open-ended choices for tasks.

I recall being a part of an elementary, school-based teacher training project a number of years ago. In cooperation with the local school district, the university where I taught was establishing an open-concept, continuous-progress learning environment. It was a brand-new school building with large open classrooms built in circle-shaped clusters. The idea was to have all the children move through various teaching stations over the course of the day, utilizing the many regular teaching staff, university professors, student teachers, and aids.

All of this looked good on paper. Much of the funding was from a special grant, and so many of the ideas came from the pen of a professor in the ivory tower of the university. The reality was that the school was located in a part of town where 40 percent of the school population would change during the course of the school year. Most of the children came from economically disadvantaged families. Many of the homes represented by these students had economic, emotional, and domestic turmoil, as well as problems with drugs and abuse. I'm sure many of these students would have qualified as ADHD if we had been looking for it.

Can you imagine the chaos of those first few days? Here was the cream of the district teaching staff, experienced professors, and lots of university students trying to get these hundreds of hyperactive, rambunctious, disrespectful elementary students to tolerate this unstructured environment. It was a disaster. After only a couple of days, there were hurriedly called staff meetings at each teaching level. At the beginning of the second week of school, the large folding doors dividing the rooms were pulled shut and individual classrooms were formed. Team-teaching efforts were put on hold. And what we had was a very structured, traditional set of classrooms, conducting business in a very methodical manner.

These children had no experience in unstructured settings. They needed clear directions, limits on their actions, and predictable sequences. It was just too unrealistic to expect them to handle the new system. I might add that by Christmas things had smoothed out, and most of the team-teaching and modified open-concept classrooms were operating as designed.

Open classrooms of the type we had proposed to use, where students accept greater responsibility for their own learning and work schedule, are usually very difficult settings for the ADHD child. A teacher who consistently follows children's behavior with appropriate consequences, both positive and negative, is likely to be the best match for your child. Classroom routines and definite consequences will help keep the child headed in the right direction.

It is helpful if the classroom environment is as uncluttered as possible. The ADHD child should not be placed in a seat directly facing the most creative and colorful bulletin boards in the room. Nor should he be looking right at the globe, windows, or that great communal gathering place of all class-rooms—the pencil sharpener. Usually, placement in the front of the classroom is appropriate. This way most of the visual distractions will be behind the student. On the other hand, if the child is seated right next to the teacher's desk there can be distractions when the rest of the students drop off their papers or come for help. The goal is to be near the source of instruction. Since many teachers move around the room while teaching, this may allow the ADHD child to have a direct line to the teacher, but away from the major dis-tractors. An individual seat, as opposed to a common table, would work best, unless this calls undo attention to the child.

Specific Educational Interventions
In this section, you will find three types of appropriate in-tervention.

● *Child-centered interventions.* These interventions are designed to aid the child in self-management. The goal is to help him develop skills to overcome problems of incompetence. We hope for success in terms of long-range, observable changes in behavior, as a result of the interventions.

Child-Centered Interventions[7]

1. Provide simple, single directions and seek feedback from the child.
2. Repeat directions as needed. Reinforce when child is doing a good job.
3. Ask the student to state classroom rules out loud. Also have the student periodically explain rules of a specific situation.
4. Encourage self-directed speech where the child stops, considers what he is going to do, and listens to himself talk about the problem and possible solutions. This is a "stop and think" or slow-down procedure.
5. Allow the child to provide his own schedule and pacing for work completion, rather than to have an imposed timetable. Teach the child to structure work and divide larger tasks into small parts.
6. Provide external visual or auditory cues to prompt continued attention and task completion.

This last idea of external visual or auditory cues to help prompt the child to maintain academic concentration has been taken to the level of hi-tech gadgetry. The Attention Training System (ATS) has been developed to serve this purpose. This involves placing on the student's desk a small, electronic module with a counter and a red light which the child knows as "Mr. Attention." The child is told that Mr. Attention will automatically award a point every minute that he or she pays attention to classroom assignments. At the end of the session, the child can convert earned points to some type of reward. This could be extra time at the computer, free time in the art area, extra recess, or other such rewarding activities. However, if the child fails to attend to task, the teacher can, from anywhere in the room, press a button on a small module. This causes a red light to shine on the student's module and a point is deducted from the accumulated total. This allows the teacher to deliver systematic and immediate feedback from anywhere in the room, without having to speak to the child or reset a timer.

This technique incorporates both positive reward and response cost. It has been shown to be as effective as stimulant medication in increasing attention to academic activities. It has allowed students to remain in the regular classroom, where otherwise they would have had to receive resource or self-contained classroom placement. The teacher is able to exert greater supervision of the ADHD student without using inordinate amounts of time and energy. The teacher can control four different student modules with one unit. Children like the ATS because reinforcement for good behavior is automatic and delivered by means of a computerlike gadget.[2]

I have used a system much like the ATS and can verify its utility in helping maintain on-task behavior. If you wish to try a nonmedication alternative for increasing attention, this is a realistic option. The unit is battery operated and sells for around $300. It can be purchased from the A.D.D. Ware-House or from Gordon Systems, Inc.

Cassettes can be used in a similar fashion. When the child hears a beep on the tape, he marks on a form if he was paying attention. The beeps can be set to sound at intermittent intervals, so the child doesn't know when the next beep will sound. The tape might be too distracting for classroom use, but could be used for training sessions at home and for homework.

● *Teacher-centered interventions.* These interventions are designed to manipulate the environment and thereby make it easier for the child to function. While they lead to immediate, effective management, they may not facilitate long-term improvements in problems of incompetence when the interventions are no longer used.[3]

Teacher-Centered Interventions

1. Maintain close contact with parents.
2. ADHD children move most easily from formal to

informal, focused to unfocused, or structured to unstructured settings.

3. Academic tasks should be well matched to the child's abilities.

4. Pace the assignments or seat work to fit the current ability of the child to complete it successfully. Several shortened work periods will be more productive.

5. Place the child in least distractible part of classroom, usually near the teacher.

6. Provide a constant classroom setting and routine. But within that routine use a combination of interesting tasks and occasional rewards.

7. Increase novelty and interest level of tasks through use of sense stimulation (e.g., color, shape, texture, sound).

8. Vary presentation format and task material. Utilize different modalities. Intersperse low and high interest tasks.

9. Supplement classroom instruction with direct instruction, drill of important academic skills, or computer-assisted instructional programs.

10. Schedule most important academic subjects during the morning hours.

11. Allow and tolerate some movement and restlessness, as long as the child is completing work.

12. Provide as much immediate feedback and teacher attention as possible.

13. Use positive reinforcement freely and often. Make sure the reward is meaningful to the student and the requirements are within the child's ability to complete.

14. Learn to use negative reinforcement (the child responds appropriately to escape or avoid a negative consequence such as the teacher's admonishment) more effectively through differential attention and reinforcement.

15. Be positive. Tell the student what you do want to have happen, rather than what you do not want to have happen.

16. Use multiple reinforcers for hierarchies of desired

behavior and ask the student his opinion about favorite reinforcers.

17. Use response cost system where the student loses previously established rewards when he exhibits inappropriate behavior.

18. Encourage use of cognitive self-control interventions where the student learns to think differently and therein modify his own behavior.

19. End interactions with the student successfully. Have the student try again, succeed, and be praised. This needs to happen often.

20. Prepare the student for changes in routine by forecasting and announcement.

21. Success in the child will come as much from adjustments in the expectations of the teacher as from other interventions.

22. Help the teacher anticipate potential problems and develop preventive strategies. This includes education of new teachers at beginning of school year.[8]

● *Parent-centered interventions.* The parents play a significant role in the child's achievement at school. The ideal parent isn't very different from the ideal teacher. The ideal home is much like the ideal classroom. All the basic principles which apply to managing an ADHD child in the classroom also work at home. These oft-repeated principles include: structure (where have we heard that before?), consistency, and immediacy of feedback over time and among adults, choosing battles, adapting the environment to compensate for disorganization and impulsiveness, and making sure that the child has a chance of succeeding. The following parent-centered interventions focus on school-related skills.

Parent-Centered Interventions

1. Maintain close contact with the classroom teacher.
2. Regarding homework:
   –Have the student check materials before leaving school.

–Use a written assignment sheet and organized system of keeping track of work.

–Parents review assignment sheet daily.

–Use a calendar for long-term projects.

–Have a quiet place and regular homework time.

–Parents monitor homework completion.

–Privileges are contingent upon doing homework.

–Materials are checked before leaving home for school.

–Implement procedures to encourage self-management of above ideas.

3. Help the child get organized. The need is for structure and more structure.

4. The student's approach to study should match the type of test questions.

5. Implement home/school report card system on daily or weekly basis to monitor progress.[9]

There are many ways to implement the daily or weekly report card. The basic components are: an *identification of the specific school-related behaviors* that are being monitored. There can be both "uppers" and "downers," preferably some of both, with an emphasis on the positive (remember, "uppers" are appropriate behaviors that the child should do more often, while "downers" are inappropriate behaviors that should be happening less often); *a system of record-keeping* that is simple, yet effective in monitoring the student's behavior on a daily basis; *a reward system* for improvement of the student's study and school-related behavior.

The following form is an example of what can be used to communicate the student's performance on a given day. It takes only a minute or two to complete.

The specific behaviors can be changed to suit the needs of your child. You can specify rewards for high-point days, as well as loss of points for low-point days. Rewards can be based on weekly improvement or on the total points for a week. A response cost arrangement can be used where a weekly reward is established. Let's say it is two dollars or two hours of TV time on the weekend. Every day the report

---

Daily Report Card

Teacher: Please rate each behavior using a point system from the following scale:

    0. Did not have a good day.
    1. Had a good day.
    2. Had a very good day.

Child's name: _____ Date: _____

Behavior:
1. Completed homework   _____
2. Completed seatwork   _____
3. Listened to instruction   _____
4. Cooperated with classroom rules   _____

                   Total   _____

---

card comes home with ones or twos, nothing is lost. But if there are any zeros, twenty-five cents or fifteen minutes is subtracted from the reward. Each day's transaction needs to be recorded or visualized in some way. A jar of marbles or tally marks on a paper will serve the purpose. By the end of the week, the child will receive whatever amount of reward remains. This type of strategy seems to work well with most ADHD children.

The School and Medication
The school should be informed if your child is on medication or trying new doses. The teacher will be asked to provide regular feedback on the child's classroom behavior and academic achievement. This information is crucial in determining the medication's effectiveness. The physician or clinician

will provide the rating forms to be used in evaluating the student's behavior. Explain how important the accurate and timely completion of these forms is to the outcome of the decision. At the outset, you should explain the monitoring process. If a double-blind study is used, the teacher will not know which protocol is being employed. Make it clear that you need to hear from the teacher if he or she notices any alarming behaviors such as twitches or social withdrawal. Also convey to the school personnel that you are desirous of using medication if it proves beneficial, but that you know all other special educational services are also needed. The school should not be allowed to expect that medication is going to solve all your child's problems, and thus assume that the educational program can remain unchanged.

When a child continues on medication, the teacher should continue to look for things such as in-seat activity, improvements in handwriting and organization on paper, decreased impulsiveness, and a higher frustration tolerance. Also, the teacher needs to be observant of differences in behavior at different times of day to help in adjustments to dosage. It is important to report any side effects such as irritability, sadness that may approach or mimic depression, increased restlessness, and excessive talkativeness.

The teacher should also be encouraged not to make statements to the child such as, "You are having a bad afternoon. Did you forget to take your pill?" Medication does not make a child "good." Pronouncements such as, "You're such a good boy when you take your medicine," should be avoided.

If a midday dosage is required, you will also have to work out the mechanics of the process. Some children are reliable enough to carry a pill in their lunch bag or pocket and take it at the appropriate time. Most need some kind of structure or reminder to maintain consistency. It might be necessary to have the school nurse dispense it, although this can be awkward for the child to have to parade up to the nurse's office every day.

For many years, school will remain a significant concern. Yet, you will gain more confidence and encouragement as you see the fruits of your efforts. It is an ongoing process, but one where you can see very definite payoff in your child's attitude, academic achievement, and relationship to teachers and classmates.

Questions about School Related Issues

1. What happens when my child goes to middle school or junior high? Is it going to be a disaster with several different teachers and classrooms?

It is possible you might have a few nightmares contemplating your child's move to the secondary grades. When your child has had trouble coping with one teacher in grade school, the prospect of six different teachers and classrooms can cause you anxiety.

Generally, this hasn't been as big a problem as you might think. The variety of teachers and the different classrooms help break up the day. This often provides the ADHD student with sufficient change of pace. It can end up being more help than hindrance.

The challenge is one of communication. Now there are several teachers with whom to coordinate homework assignments. A school counselor is an important source of coordination and communication at the junior high and senior high levels.

It is true that some secondary teachers are relatively close-minded and inflexible in regard to teaching style and classroom conduct. You may need to do some one-on-one education and rapport building to help your child's teachers understand the difference between noncompliance and incompetency.

The all-important assignment notebook will probably need to be chained to your child's belt, and there will still need to be frequent progress reports between you and the teachers. Supplementary services such as resource room should still be available, if needed. While middle school is a challenge, it can be a continued time of growth and maturity.

2. What can I do about helping my child develop friendships with his classmates?

The core problems of impulsivity, overactivity, and inattention give rise to many of the peer problems that ADHD children experience. Their impulsivity can lead them to lash out in aggression when they are challenged or become angry. Their overactivity can put them out of sync with children who prefer a slower pace. Their inattention may cause difficulties when they are playing games that require following rules or keeping track of what is happening.

Treatment of the core problems, as described in previous chapters, can help relieve some of the difficulties your child has with his peers and classmates. There will still need to be focused and specific instruction on how to make and keep friends. The social-skills training classes mentioned earlier can help. However, these skills do not end up being used outside of class unless the parents reinforce and model the skills of friendship. For example, the ADHD child is not alert to the social cues that are obvious to his peers. A raised eyebrow, a pause, or a pointed look escapes notice, and so he easily misses important signals available to more socially astute onlookers.

You can try to structure your child's environment to maximize his likelihood of developing good social skills. You might allow him to invite over one friend at a time. Your child needs only one reciprocal friendship, as opposed to numerous friends. Think carefully about the person you allow to come over. Children with good social skills may be able to model appropriate behavior for your child. In addition, you should plan activities that offer structure to the children's interactions. You may want to remain present during their playtime to supervise these activities.

Talk with your child ahead of time, letting him know exactly what you expect. If he is bossy, explain to him how to let his friend go first in a game. Role play and suggest a game plan that will help your child remember to share or take turns. Create a secret sign, like a wink, that will let your child know you notice his attempts to use his new skills. You may also need to gently pull your child aside to offer suggestions on how to act from time to time. Avoid criticizing him in front of his playmate.

You can serve as a model for your child on how to develop a friendship. Be nice to your child's friends. Go out of your way to make them feel welcome in your home. Try to make your home a fun place to be so that other children want to come over. You cannot make friends for your child, but you can encourage the kinds of interactions that will help your child establish friendships.

Keep the playtime short at first. Let the other child leave while they are still having fun. Monitor the children as they play, and reward your child's appropriate behavior. If hostilities begin to arise, intervene early. Stop the aggression before it has a chance to develop.

Be realistic about friendship. For many children, friendships are transient and change from year to year. When your child finds one or two good friends, promote those relationships, but do not be surprised when the connections cool off. Just be alert to how you can encourage transitions to new friendships.[5, 6]

References

1. United States Department of Education, "Clarification of Policy to Address the Needs of Children with Attention Deficit Disorders within General and/or Special Education" (Washington, D.C.: Office of Special Education and Rehabilitative Services, 1991).

2. Gordon, M., *ADHD/Hyperactivity: A Consumer's Guide* (DeWitt, New York: GSI Publications, 1991).

3. Goldstein, S., and Goldstein, M., *Managing Attention Disorders in Children* (New York: John Wiley & Sons, 1990).

4. Goldstein, S., and Goldstein, M., "The Multi-Disciplinary Evaluation and Treatment of Children with Attention Deficit Disorders," 16th ed. (Salt Lake City: Neurology, Learning and Behavior Center, 1991).

5. Bain, L.J., *Attention-Deficit Disorders* (New York: Dell Publishing, 1991).

6. Garber, S.W., Garber, M.D., and Spizman, R.F., *If Your Child Is Hyperactive, Inattentive, Impulsive, Distractible . . . Helping the ADD Hyperactive Child* (New York: Villard Books, 1990).

7. Adapted from Goldstein and Goldstein, *Managing Attention Disorders in Children,* pages 315–317, Copyright 1990. Used by permission of authors and publisher.

8. Adapted from Goldstein and Goldstein, *The Multi-Disciplinary Evaluation and Treatment of Children with Attention Deficit Disorders,* pages 78–80, Copyright 1991. Used by permission of authors and publisher.

9. Some items adapted from Goldstein and Goldstein, *The Multi-Disciplinary Evaluation and Treatment of Children with Attention Deficit Disorders,* pages 74–75, Copyright 1991. Used by permission of authors and publisher.

ChAPTER EiGHT

HOW CAN GOD HELP?
Spiritual Issues
in ADHD Treatment

Not long ago a little boy with ADHD asked his mother, "Mom, why can't something be wrong with my arm and not my brain?" Later he added, "You can't fix my brain."

You may have had the same question, along with, "Why *my* child? Is this God's punishment for a sin of the past?" or "Why would God allow this to happen?"

I certainly don't have the answers to these questions, any more than I would claim to understand the mind and purposes of God. But I do believe ADHD children have every potential for creative and fulfilled lives. There is ample reason to be optimistic about their ability to mature, yield fruit in season, and prosper in whatever they do (Psalm 1:3).

Parenting is difficult with any child, and even more challenging when a child has special needs. That is why the spiritual resources available to a Christian parent can make all the difference in the world. You don't have to face this task alone or with only your own strength and understanding. You have God's promise of direction and power. If part of God's purpose is to help a parent develop patience, then blessing you with a child with attention deficit is a guaranteed way to meet that goal.

The Grief Process

Every loss brings with it the phases of grief. Grief can be thought of as a mourning process in which a person gradually becomes *reoriented to life* without the former place, value, person, experience, or possession. This process usually proceeds through certain distinct phases which are not always sequential. You may bounce back and forth between the phases. Even with the variations, however, these phases can be a way to track how you are adjusting or reorienting to life with a changed perspective.

The grief process certainly is true for adjusting to life with an ADHD child. You already knew things were stressful; the diagnosis just gave you a name and a process for coping with and managing the situation. The grief process allows you to adjust to a clearer understanding of your child's needs.

• *Phase one.* When you first identified that your child has ADHD, you may have experienced the initial feelings of doubt, *disbelief,* and denial. Your thoughts might have included, "No, it's not true. The doctor made a mistake. This is just a passing thing—he'll grow out of it." This initial *shock* phase of grief includes the same feelings you have when a tragic message is conveyed. You don't want to believe it is true. Your heart and soul cry out against the possibility of the trauma. You might even strike out against the bearer of the message. "The doctor is crazy. I'll go somewhere else and get a second opinion." These are common reactions to the initial shock or unexpected pronouncement, such as learning that your child has attention deficit.

• *Phase two.* After the initial shock come feelings of *anger,* rage, and fear. "Why can't the doctors figure this out? What's wrong with those experts that they can't find a cure? Where is God? This is all so unfair. We already had more problems than we could handle, and now this. How are we going to manage? I don't think I can take any more."

Such feelings tend to emerge during the anger phase of grief. You may harbor anger at God because He let you down. "Why does my child have to struggle with these problems? Why hasn't God answered my prayers?"

I cannot deny the pain, and I cannot explain why such things happen. I just know God can work and be glorified even in the middle of our problems. He understands our anger. The process of raising an ADHD child to health and maturity is a tedious journey, not an overnight trip. The process of identifying your fear and anger will take a while. But as the journey proceeds, you will find anger and doubt turning to hope.

The change from doubt to hope happens, in part, because of *where* you place your faith. That's why a portion of faith the size of a mustard seed is sufficient. If you look to yourself for all of the answers in handling a difficult child, you will be disappointed, frustrated, and continually angry. That is the wrong place to put your belief. By placing it in God, you are assured of help and healing (Psalm 37:5; James 1:5).

God accepts you in the process of dealing with your anger and learning to believe. A father once asked Jesus if He could heal his son who had an evil spirit. Jesus replied, "Everything is possible for him who believes." Immediately the boy's father exclaimed, "I do believe; help me overcome my unbelief!" Then Jesus proceeded to cast out the evil spirit and the boy was made whole (see Mark 9:14-27). The process of grief will include times of anger and doubt. The exciting thing is that God will accept you even in your angry and doubting state.

● *Phase three.* Following the spells of anger, you may experience intermittent periods of *false hope* or deal-making. This is when you may be tempted to invest in quick cures and unproven treatment programs. You want to believe with all your heart that your son or daughter can be "normal" and not have to struggle with the problems of inattention and distractibility.

During this phase, some parents look to spiritual or quasimedical promises for elimination of the problem. I wish they worked. I readily acknowledge God's power; I know that He can heal anything, including ADHD. But I worry about the feelings of a child who did nothing to deserve the problems of ADHD in the first place. Now he might have to endure unfruitful spiritual interventions which come up empty. The tendency will be for that child to internalize the blame and conclude it is his fault that he wasn't cured.

I think it is more realistic to acknowledge the presently incurable nature of ADHD and focus on the methods of intervention that have been shown to be helpful. Included in those interventions are spiritual resources, including prayer. However, I ask you to be discerning and cautious about creating false hope.

The *deal-making* part of grieving occurs when you promise God you will make changes in your life *if* God will heal your child. If God convicts you to make necessary additions or deletions to your life, by all means be obedient to that call. I just don't believe a child's health should be made a bargaining chip in that process. God isn't in the business of authoring illness to bring us to repentance. Periods of hardship, including illness of a family member, can result in life-changing commitments, but those are by-products of God's grace. It was not that God caused the original problem. It is that He is great enough to work His ways, in spite of the problem.

• *Phase four.* The next phase of mourning comes in the form of a dark cloud of *depression* and feelings of gloom, pessimism, and guilt. Things haven't changed dramatically for the better. You have sought professional opinion, enlisted the prayers of your church, and your child still overreacts and is impulsive. You begin to believe things will never be resolved. Your child will grow up with significant emotional problems. And it will all be your fault. These are the misbeliefs of this phase.

There is hope. Your child can be helped. God will be with you. True, reality is showing you that the struggle is enduring, but this doesn't mean you are failing. It just means that you need large doses of both patient love and tough love.

• *Phase five.* At this point *acceptance* begins to take hold. You realize that the problems are significant, but that the resources of God working through you are unlimited. The flesh will be weak at times. Your heart will be weary and heavy. However, prudent management, diligent enforcement, constant teaching, and the ever-present structure, are starting to pay dividends. You begin to see changes in your child. The school reports are a bit better. A few friends call to come over and play. There is hope. The reorientation has begun to take hold.

Spiritual Foundations for Parenting

If parenting any child is worth a college education, then raising an ADHD child should give you a Ph.D. The task is continuous and the challenge is great. Our spiritual foundation gives the Christian father and mother a basis to claim a victory, even when the progress reports are discouraging. In this section I want to review our basic position between God and our children and apply it to the special needs of a child with attention deficit.

As Christians we are part of a royal priesthood (1 Peter 2:9). The priesthood of all believers means that each Christian has personal access to God. Each of us can approach God on behalf of another. We are to declare the praises of Him who called us out of darkness into light.

This has great implications for parents. We are called and ordained by God as priests for our children. This relationship involves two basic positions that we see symbolized in a liturgical form of worship. The first position is when the minister or priest faces the people, speaking to the congregation on behalf of God. The second position is when the minister or priest faces the altar, speaking to God on behalf of the people. Our responsibility to our children takes these same positions. We are called to *present God to our children* through our actions and words. We are also called to continually *present our children to God* in prayer.

One mandate for Christian parenting is found in Deuteronomy 6:4-9. This passage points out both of the positions we are to fill between God and our children.

Hear, O Israel: The Lord our God, the Lord is one. Love

the Lord your God with all your heart and with all your soul and with all your strength. These commandments that I give you today are to be upon your hearts. Impress them on your children. Talk about them when you sit at home and when you walk along the road, when you lie down and when you get up. Tie them as symbols on your hands and bind them on your foreheads. Write them on the doorframes of your houses and on your gates.

Christian parenting is based on our faith in God. We are to first love God with our whole being. The rest of the injunctions follow from that requirement. This passage suggests that we have four means of presenting God to our children and one means of presenting our children to God.

• *Example.* The first way we present God to our children is by our *example.* We are to "impress" our children in matters of faith and of life. We do this by action as well as word (1 Kings 9:4; 2 Chronicles 17:3; 2 Timothy 1:5). The old saying, "Do as I say, not as I do," simply does not work. A child will follow the example he sees every day much more than the lectures he hears about how and why he should act in certain ways. This tremendous influence starts with day one. If a teenager has received years of criticism from his parents, the effects are not going to disappear overnight.

Our example before our children should include the full range of human emotions. Reality tells us there will be days of sadness and anger, as well as days of happiness and joy. A child does not need to be privy to all the innermost feelings of his parents. But he needs to see that a Christian can mourn a loss, feel anger over frustrations, and yet work through those events with the grace and strength of God. Our children need to see that victorious Christian living is not accomplished by eliminating all our problems. Rather, it is achieved by allowing God to work His wonders in spite of our problems.

The ADHD child encounters many frustrations. He knows very early that life can be difficult. The message we want to convey is that we serve a God who will show His power in spite of our weaknesses. The parallel of life to the presence of ADHD is clear: ADHD will not go away; life contains its inevitable problems. We have a chance to show our children that we do our very best to cope with life, and then learn to glorify God as He works through our weaknesses (2 Corinthians 12:9-10).

A child's image of God is greatly influenced by parental example. The way we set forth a standard of conduct, behavior, and worship toward God will guide our children toward an ability to see God in their lives. Our children begin to understand that God is real and vital when they see that God is authentic and active in our lives. We have said that an ADHD child needs repeated exposure to hands-on learning experiences with immediate feedback; he needs the same repetition of spiritual example. Our children should see and hear daily evidence of our faith in action.

• *Words.* The second form of influence is through the *words* of our mouths. This is the *instruction* or teaching we provide. We are to "talk" about our love of God, our beliefs and values, and why they are important (Proverbs 22:6; Colossians 3:16; 2 Timothy 3:15). Deuteronomy 4:9 instructs us, "Teach them to your children and to their children after them." Our instruction is to be diligent and pervasive. Instruction is to take place whether we are walking in the park, fishing on a lake, or kneeling down for bedtime prayers. This instruction can be informal as well as formal. It occurs during the chat while riding in the pickup to the hardware store. Stories told at dinnertime can have a lasting impact, as well as the instruction given over devotions or at family meetings. Sometimes the message appears to be going in one ear and out the other. But parental instruction, whether direct or indirect, guides many of the values, attitudes, opinions, and beliefs of our children. We should talk with them about their activities, so that they realize these are to be undertaken with care and thoughtfulness.

Another form of presenting God to children is seen in verses 8 and 9 of Deuteronomy 6. We see that *pictures* and *symbols,* or the many nonverbal or aesthetic forms of communication and expression, are important ways to communicate truths about God. The way we decorate our homes can either intensify or dull an awareness of God and Jesus. We have many symbols in the church—the cross, a lamb, the alpha and omega, three intertwined circles, a Nativity scene, and various pictures or artistic renditions of religious themes. All of these objects communicate the importance of our faith and should have a place of prominence. Think back over your own life. How many sermon outlines do you remember? How many illustrations, stories, word pictures, or life experiences can you recall? Many of our recollections will contain pictures and scenes as the component of lasting spiritual influence. Be sure to draw on this source of influence for the benefit of your children.

● *Consequences.* The next form of parental impact takes place through *consequences.* The commandments mentioned in verse 6 were subject to the consequences of God's discipline. Likewise, parents are to exercise loving authority with their children (Proverbs 19:18; 23:13-14; 29:15, 17). In earlier chapters I have discussed many ways to apply consequences. You will need to draw on both positive and negative consequences. Remember to put more deposits in the relationship account than withdrawals. The ratio of positive experiences to negative events needs to be at least four to one.

This category of consequences is very practical and beneficial because it parallels the discipline of God. There are negative consequences for sin and there are positive fruits for obedience. We present part of the plan of God as we apply consequences to the actions of our children. Learn to use it effectively.

● *Prayer.* The final injunction to parents is to present our children to God in *prayer.* We read about Abraham praying for Ishmael (Genesis 17:18), David praying for the life of his child (2 Samuel 12:16) and for Solomon (1 Chronicles 29:19). The first chapter of Job tells us how Job made sacrifices and prayers for his children (Job 1:5). Scripture describes several New Testament parents who petitioned Christ for the benefit of their children (Matthew 17:15; Mark 7:26).

As parents we are to continually pray for our children as we present them to God. In addition we are to teach them to pray. We are to petition God for their spiritual and physical well-being.

Types of Prayer

There are different kinds of prayers presented in Scripture.

● There are prayers of *confession* (Ezra 10:11; 2 Chronicles 7:14; 1 John 1:9; James 5:16). As you deal with the frustrations and aggravations of raising an ADHD child, there may be times when your patience runs thin and you respond in ways that are unhealthy or destructive. Words of anger, criticism, even discipline in overly punitive ways, may emerge. Later you will feel convicted and go to God in confession and repentance. The magnificent grace of God extends to any and all errors of parenting you may make. Take your confession to Him and He will relieve the burden.

● All Christian parents have sought God's *guidance* in a desire to do the right thing in raising our children. Prayers seeking God's guidance are very important (2 Samuel 2:1; 1 Chronicles 14:14; Psalms 5:8; 143:10). He has promised to give us direction for all aspects of our lives. This certainly includes the nurturing and correction of a child with attention deficit.

Your prayer can be like that of Jesus as He sought His Father's will, "Your will be done on earth as it is in heaven" (Matthew 6:10). For it is only God who can bring about the miracle of a transformed life. Praying for the knowledge of God's will and the power to carry it out helps you set aside selfish motives. Through prayer you can receive reassurance of God's presence and know He wants your child to lead a healthy and productive life.

Guidance will also come from the reading of God's Word. It is important to spend time in Scripture with the purpose of letting His truths speak to you. Scripture is a lamp to your feet (Psalm 119:105). It is food to help you grow (1 Peter 2:2). God's Word is a life-giving force (Ezekiel 37:1-14). It has the power to save (Romans 1:16). Scripture gives hope (Romans 15:4), and it will help probe and illuminate your specific needs (Hebrews 4:12). I don't believe one can spend time in Scripture with the specific intent of having God speak to you, and have that time prove fruitless. This applies to your personal life as well as to the task of parenting your child.

• Closely related to guidance are prayers for *wisdom* (2 Chronicles 1:10; Psalm 90:12; Ephesians 1:17; Colossians 1:9). Wisdom is more than knowledge of basic facts and principles. It is the application of understandings in prudent and thoughtful ways that reflect discernment and spiritual comprehension. It certainly requires the wisdom of Solomon to know when to correct an ADHD child for noncompliance rather than to instruct him for incompetent behavior. It takes experience with the child in order to make these distinctions, and it takes wisdom to know the best ways of communicating. Basic techniques and strategies, such as those found in this book, are helpful places to begin. But your requests for holy insight can make all the difference in the world.

• There are certainly prayers of *thanksgiving* in the lives of every Christian (Deuteronomy 8:10; Psalm 100:4; Colossians 1:12; 1 Thessalonians 5:18). God will answer your prayers in some form. You will see your children pass milestones of development. Seemingly insurmountable problems will be resolved. Then it is most important to thank God for His mercy and answers to your petitions.

• At the same time, God is to be approached through prayers of *adoration* (Psalms 21:13; 47:9; 57:11; 108:5; Acts 4:24; 16:25). He is awesome and worthy to be praised. God is to be exalted above all things. Our children need to see and hear our praises directed to God for the blessings He bestows on all of His children.

• There can also be prayers of *meditation* (Psalms 4:4; 19:14; 104:34; 119:99). These are times when we search our hearts for answers to life's vexing problems. We dwell on the Word of God and ask it to be made real and alive in our daily lives. This is the essence of meditation. We examine the precepts of God and consider His ways as they relate to coping with the demands of an ADHD child. The result is insight that transcends the mere teaching of men. Meditation and prayer open our eyes to the richness of God's teaching and direction for our lives.

• There are certainly times when parents will need to

convey prayers of *intercession* to God on behalf of our children. Just as Jesus through the work of the Holy Spirit intercedes for us, so we petition God for the needs of our children (Luke 22:32; John 14:16; 17:9). Sometimes our intercession is for their very salvation and eternal destiny. At other times, you may approach the throne of God for success in school or friendships for your ADHD child.

You may also need to have periods of prayer and fasting (Joel 2:12; Matthew 6:18; Acts 14:23). This is valuable when you confront serious obstacles in your child's progress toward health and maturity. It gives a time of focus and concentration for your prayers and sharpens your ability to pray for specific needs and concerns for your child.

• As Satan is more direct in his warfare within our culture, there will be an increasing need for prayers of *deliverance* (2 Kings 19:19; Psalm 91:3; Luke 8:31-32; 2 Corinthians 1:10; 2 Timothy 4:18; 2 Peter 2:9). Our children may fall into bondage, sin, or demonic attack. It takes the mighty name of Jesus Christ through His shed blood on the cross and the power of the Almighty God to confound and defeat the wily ways of Satan. But there is no question about the eventual winner in the claim for our eternal lives. God will triumph in the battle for our children, including the struggles of an ADHD child. But there may be times when we need to call on the warriors of heaven and light to help us fend off the entanglements of the prince of darkness.

• In the rush of daily schedules and demands, there are times when *short arrow prayers* are all we can do to contact God about a particular issue (Nehemiah 2:4; Ecclesiastes 5:2). This is perfectly acceptable. In fact, God has instructed us to keep our prayers short and to the point. If we pray only to hear ourselves or to impress others, God will not hear us. Maybe you are in the process of correcting your child right in the middle of the produce section at the grocery store. Time and circumstance won't allow a bended knee or lengthy discourse with God. You simply utter a request for guidance and go on with your discipline. When we have an ongoing communion and relationship with God, we don't have to spend twenty minutes giving the spiritual passwords to gain His attention. He is there immediately whenever we need Him.

Prayer is a pretty simple activity. Your prayers do not need to be wordy or complex. A simple expression of adoration for God, followed by statements of confession, need, and thankfulness, is sufficient. The Lord's Prayer is a perfect model (Matthew 6:9-13; Luke 11:2-4).

I know you may have called out to God in times of crises and wondered if He would ever answer. Why does your child have to struggle with problems of inattention, low self-esteem, and conflict with family members? All of us have had feelings of being abandoned and ignored. Biblical heroes such as Jeremiah and David expressed the same feelings. But God has made some rather remarkable promises, and He does not lie. Here are a few of those promises:

- God will answer our prayers (Mark 11:24).
- God has never failed to keep His promises (1 Kings 8:56).
- God has guaranteed to be faithful (Deuteronomy 7:9; 1 Corinthians 1:9).
- God will deliver us from afflictions (Psalms 30:5; 41:3).
- God knows our limits (Isaiah 43:2; 1 Corinthians 10:13).
- God will comfort us in hard times (Isaiah 43:1).
- God will help remove obstacles (Luke 17:6).

Biblical Principles for Structure

The ADHD child needs consistent structure. All children do. It's just that the ADHD child needs more of it, and for a longer period of time. To this end, in earlier chapters I have described many examples of structure that can apply to your child. The principles underlying these techniques are identified in Scripture.

● The first principle is *clarity* (Matthew 5:37). Because you are competing with a distractible and inattentive nature, you should make your instructions clear and simple. When you tell your child no, you should act accordingly. It only makes the problem worse if an ADHD child learns that if he badgers Mom long enough, she will eventually give in. Make your rules and stick to them unless there is clear reason to change. The rules and consequences for violating those rules should be spelled out clearly. Rewards for success should be equally clear.

• The second principle is *consistency* (Psalm 15:4). This verse talks about a man keeping his word. There are two types of consistency that affect an ADHD child. The first is the need for both parents to enforce the same expectations, to the same degree, from day to day and week after week. This is consistency over *time*. No one does this perfectly, but the goal is to be as reliable as possible.

The second aspect of consistency is *between parents and other caretakers*. Dad should enforce the rules to the same degree that mother enforces the rules. The day-care environment should be similar to the expectations you apply at home. An ADHD child cannot handle a wide variation between the disciplinary styles of his parents or between home and school. Everyone needs to work for as much uniformity as possible in all the *places* in your child's life.

Avoid making promises you aren't sure you can keep. It may be better not to say anything about a future event, if you aren't sure it will happen. For example, you may want to take your child to the indoor playground that just opened near the shopping center. If Dad doesn't have to work overtime this coming Saturday, the family can probably go. It's better to wait until you know for sure that Dad is available before telling your child. Otherwise, you will have to deal with the overreactive outburst of feelings when Dad calls and says he has to work Saturday.

• *Regularity* is the third principle we see in Scripture that applies to the ADHD child (2 Timothy 1:5). Just as Timothy saw sincere faith in his mother and grandmother, so parents today are to be diligent, persistent, and regular. ADHD children are demanding. Patience will run out. Cross words will be spoken, and grace must be extended again and again. But that is just what the child needs. Repeatedly *tell* your child you love him, and then *show* it on a regular and continuing basis.

• Another idea we see in Scripture is the importance of *enforceability* (Ecclesiastes 8:11). Consequences, whether positive or negative, need to be applied immediately for the best effect. Parents should not make idle threats. If you can't carry out a threat, don't make it (Proverbs 29:20). I have heard of statements like, "Behave yourself or I'll kick you out of the car and make you walk home." There is no way a responsible parent is going to make a six-year-old child walk the busy streets or lonely country road back to their house. Hasty comments are harmful. ADHD children have trouble using rules and abstract values to control their behavior. They are more governed by the immediate. So parents need to enforce rules immediately. Do not say, "Wait till your father gets home." The child will have forgotten what the consequence was all about, and the effect will be lost.

• Finally, we see the principle of *fairness* (Genesis 25:28; 37:3). These Old Testament references show the human resentment that comes when a child perceives he isn't being treated fairly. Granted, children often confuse fairness and equality. Fairness occurs when your expectations match the abilities of your child. Parents need to discuss their mutual expectations for their ADHD child. These expectations should correspond with both developmental considerations and known ADHD features.

Consider the differences between noncompliance and incompetence. It is unfair to reprimand or punish a child for doing something that is out of his control. With ADHD children, it's certainly not easy to make the distinction. But that is where experience and prayerful discernment come into action to help you "know" when to lower the boom and when to back off.

Trusting God

Being a Christian doesn't take the hard work out of raising an ADHD child. But it does give you the spiritual resources to cope with the frustrations. Another key ingredient in the process is your ability to trust God for the future of your children. This task of trusting is certainly challenged by the daily drain of coping with a child who doesn't pay attention and seems to overreact to everything in his world.

"Trust in the Lord with all your heart and lean not on your own understanding; in all your ways acknowledge Him, and

He will make your paths straight" (Proverbs 3:5-6). These verses capture the essence of your need to trust. Your finite understanding can only lead to incomplete efforts to manage yourself and your family. Trusting in God demands an affirmative decision. You must move through the veil of denial which shuts out the light of God. Your path will be illuminated and made straight by choosing to let God be your guide.

Trust happens with experience and grows over time. At this point you may be able to give God responsibility for only part of your life. That's okay. Give Him what you can. As He proves faithful in some things, you will be able to hand over more aspects of your life and your ability to parent.

Abraham is listed in the Hebrews 11 roll call of the heroes of faith. His faith did not develop overnight. Abraham was one of the Bible's greatest worriers. He worried that foreign kings would covet his beautiful wife and kill him to get her (Genesis 12:12-13; 20:11). He worried about shortages of grazing land for his animals (Genesis 13:6-8), about retaliation (Genesis 15:1), about a lack of an heir (Genesis 15:2-3), about God's possible inability to honor His covenant (Genesis 16:1-4), and about God's intent to destroy Sodom and Gomorrah (Genesis 18:23-33).

In spite of God's promises, Abraham worried that he and Sarah were too old to bear children. After the birth of Isaac, Abraham worried that God wouldn't know which of his two sons to use in fulfilling the promise of many descendants (Genesis 21:11).

It took time and experience for Abraham to become a man of faith. He grew from his experiences, just as we can. There were times Abraham took matters into his own hands, with disastrous results, just as we do. But God was patient; Abraham became obedient and learned to trust God. You can experience the same steps to belief. Be patient with yourself; yet continue to be diligent in moving toward that greater understanding of the love and mercy of the Lord.

Questions about Spiritual Issues and ADHD

1. *What kind of answers might I expect from God when I pray for my ADHD child to be healed or changed?*

I don't claim to have all of the answers for questions like this. Many good books have been written about prayer, suffering, or afflictions. These include *The Problem of Pain* by C.S. Lewis, *Where Is God When It Hurts?* by Philip Yancey, and *Affliction* by Edith Schaeffer. I have found them all helpful, but some questions seem to always remain.

I believe we can start with the assumption that there is nothing too difficult for God to change. There is no event in history that was too hard for God to miraculously alter for the good of the kingdom. He could easily have answered Jesus' cry with a complete change in circumstances. The victory of Christ on the cross is sufficient to cover any request that we might direct to God (Isaiah 53:12; John 16:33). The resurrection of Christ healed the broken relationship between God and man. This opened the way for an intimate relationship. That kinship we have with God gives us the permission to come boldly before Him with our every request (Luke 11:9; John 15:7).

Part of the reason we become frustrated with God's seeming unwillingness to answer our prayers is because of our shortsighted, time-bound, earthly perspective. God does not promise that *all* of our requests are to be answered by an immediate change in circumstance. Scripture gives us a balanced perspective about faith. The faith that allows a parent to pray for the healing of a child, and yet continue with sufficient grace to deal with the problems of daily living, is no less faith than that of a parent who utters a similar prayer and finds an immediate resolution of the problems. These are both answers to prayer. The second is more immediate and more in line with our expectations. But they both reflect God's love and grace.

I don't understand God's perspective, of course. But part of the answer to the dilemma of seemingly unanswered prayer comes from a larger view of history. The death and resurrection of Christ give complete victory. But to see this we must look at all that has taken place in history, rather than expect total victory in any one life. When we read the statement, "If you ask anything in My name, I will do it," this doesn't mean that all of our individual requests will be answered by a change in circumstance. Rather, there will be a literal fulfillment of this promise in the total collection of all the answered prayers in all of history. In some way, Satan will be defeated at every place where his devices have been attempted. In the end Christ will destroy all dominion, authority, and power but His own (1 Corinthians 15:24; Revelation 15:2; 17:14).

This means we will probably have a balance of prayers that are answered by dramatic changes of the kind we expected; some will be answered with a "wait," and our learning of patience. Still other prayers will be answered with an understanding that God's grace is sufficient during times of difficulty.

2. *How can the church help in the total intervention process for my child?*

There are several ways the church can be a resource to you and your child. The first is for the community of believers to be a source of support and encouragement for you as parents. Through Bible study groups, home meetings, and corporate fellowship, your needs for spiritual and social inspiration can be met. Take the risk to share your burden with others in the church, so they can help carry the load (Galatians 6:2).

There are practical ways your church should be able to help—baby-sitting, referral recommendations, respite care while Mom and Dad take a break, safe and secure day care, and guidance from church staff for the spiritual training of your child. Also, corporate prayer can be very important.

Ideally, the Christian education program of your church should provide a structured opportunity for your child to gain exposure to the principles of Christian living and biblical truths. The very same ideas presented earlier for classroom teachers may need to be applied to the Sunday School classroom. Your child may have been a disruptive force there before the ADHD assessment and treatment process was started. With your current understanding, take these techniques to the church context so your child is able to profit from the spiritual training offered there. Perhaps you will need to take the initiative to see that appropriate in-service training is provided to your child's teachers. The materials described earlier are appropriate to use. A Sunday School teacher or youth leader needs to have the same understanding about incompetence versus noncompliance that you and the schoolteacher have acquired. Make sure the church staff have an opportunity to learn about the special characteristics and needs of a child with attention deficit. Your goal should be to have your child experience *at least* the same amount of loving concern and appropriate structure from his church learning environment as he receives from his classroom teacher.

PART THREE

RESOURCES FOR ADHD

"So do not fear, for I am with you;
do not be dismayed, for I am your God.
I will strengthen you and help you;
I will uphold you with My righteous right hand."

(Isaiah 41:10)

ReSOURCES

Books for Parents

1. Bain, L.J., *Attention Deficit Disorders* (New York: Dell Publishing, 1991).

2. Conners, C.K., *Feeding the Brain: How Foods Affect Children* (New York: Plenum Press, 1989).

3. Fowler, M.C., *Maybe You Know My Kid* (New York: Birch Lane Press, 1990).

4. Garber, S.W., Garber, M.D., and Spizman, R.F., *If Your Child Is Hyperactive, Inattentive, Impulsive, Distractible... Helping the ADD Hyperactive Child* (New York: Villard Books, 1990).

5. Goldstein, S., and Goldstein, M., *Parent's Guide: Attention-Deficit Hyperactivity Disorder* (Salt Lake City: Neurology, Learning & Behavior Center, 1990).

6. Gordon, M., *ADHD/Hyperactivity: A Consumer's Guide* (DeWitt, New York: GSI Publications, 1991).

7. Ingersoll, B., *Your Hyperactive Child: A Parent's Guide to Coping with Attention-Deficit Disorder* (New York: Doubleday, 1988).

8. Kelley, M.L., *School-Home Notes: Promoting Children's Classroom Success* (New York: Guilford Press, 1990).

9. Loney, J., *The Young Hyperactive Child: Answers to Questions about Diagnosis, Prognosis and Treatment* (New York: The Haworth Press, 1987).

10. Maxey, D.W., *How to Own and Operate an Attention-Deficit Kid* (Roanoke, Virginia: HAAD Support Groups, P.O. Box 20563, Roanoke, VA 24018, 1989).

11. McCarney, S.B., and Bauer, A.M., *The Parent's Guide to Attention-Deficit Disorders* (Columbia, Missouri: Hawthorne. 1990).

12. Moss, R.A., *Why Johnny Can't Concentrate: Coping with Attention-Deficit Problems* (New York: Bantam Books, 1990).

13. Parker, H.C., *The ADD Hyperactivity Workbook for Parents, Teachers, and Kids* (Plantation, Florida: Impact Publications, 1988).

14. Silver, L.B., *Attention-Deficit Disorders: Booklet for Parents* (Summit, New Jersey: CIBA, 1980).

15. Taylor, J.F., *Helping Your Hyperactive Child* (Rocklin, California: Prima Publishing & Communications, 1990).

16. Wender, P.H., *The Hyperactive Child, Adolescent, and Adult* (New York: Oxford University Press, 1987).

Books for Children

1. Galvin, M., *Otto Learns about His Medicine. A Story about Medication for Hyperactive Children* (New York: Magination Press, 1988).

2. Gehret, J., *Eagle Eyes. A Child's View of Attention-Deficit Disorder* (Fairport, New York: Verbal Images Press, 1991).

3. Gordon, M., *Jumpin' Johnny. Get Back to Work. A Child's Guide to ADHD/Hyperactivity* (Dewitt, New York: GSI Publications, 1991).

4. Gordon, M., *My Brother's a World-Class Pain: A Sibling's Guide to ADHD* (Dewitt, New York: GSI Publications, 1991).

5. Moss, D.M., *Shelley, the Hyperactive Turtle* (Kesington, Maryland: Woodbine House, 1989).

6. Nadeau, K.G. & Dixon, E.B., *Learning to Slow Down and*

Pay Attention (Annandale, Virginia: Chesapeake Psychological Services, 1991).

7. Parker, R.N., *Making the Grade: An Adolescent's Struggle with ADD* (Plantation, Florida: Impact Publications, 1992).

8. Quinn, P.O., & Stern, J., *Putting on the Brakes* (New York: Magination Press, 1992).

Books for Professionals
1. Barkley, R.A., *Attention Deficit Hyperactivity Disorder. A Handbook for Diagnosis and Treatment* (New York: Guilford Press, 1990).

2. Barkley, R.A., *Defiant Children: A Clinician's Manual for Parent Training* (New York: Guilford Press, 1987).

3. Copeland, E.D., *Medications for Attention Disorders (ADHD/ADD) and Related Medical Problems* (Atlanta: SPI Press, 1991).

4. Goldstein, S., and Goldstein, M., *Managing Attention Disorders in Children* (New York: John Wiley & Sons, 1990).

5. Robin, A.L., and Foster, S.L., *Negotiating Parent-Adolescent Conflict: A Behavioral Family Systems Approach* (New York: Guilford Publications, 1989).

6. Weiss, G., & Hechtman, L.T., *Hyperactive Children Grown Up* (New York: Guilford Press, 1986).

Devotional Materials for Children
1. Johnson, A.H., & Simon, M.P., *Little Visits with God* (St. Louis: Concordia, 1957). For families with grade school children.

2. Johnson, A.H. & Simon, M.P., *More Little Visits with God* (St. Louis: Concordia, 1961). For families with young children.

3. Simon, M.M., *More Little Visits with Jesus* (St. Louis: Concordia, 1966, 1971, 1976). For families with young children.

4. Tengdon, M., *Does Anyone Care How I Feel?* (Minneapolis: Bethany House, 1981).

5. Weishett, E., *God's Love for God's Children* (Minneapolis: Augsburg Press, 1986).

6. Williamson, D., *Quiet Times with Active Preschoolers* (Minneapolis: Augsburg Press, 1989).

Resources for Teaching Social Skills

1. Walker, H.M., Todis, B., Holmes, D., & Horton, G., *The Walker Social Skills Curriculum: The ACCESS program* (Austin, Texas: Pro-Ed, 1988). Appropriate for children and adolescents. Consists of 31 sessions to be used in a small group setting. Each lesson includes a review of the previously taught skill, the introduction of the new skill, an opportunity to practice and develop an understanding of this skill through discussion and role play, and a contract in which each student makes a commitment to when and with whom the new skill will be practiced for the coming week.

2. Hazel, J.S., Bragg Schumaker, J., Sherman, J.A., & Sheldon-Wildgen, J., *Asset: A Social Skills Program for Adolescents* (Champaign, Illinois: Research Press, 1981). This is a video program for both normal and adolescents who are having significant interactional problems. There are eight videocassettes dealing with skills such as giving feedback, peer pressure, problem-solving, negotiation, following instructions and conversation. Student manuals and leader's guide are included.

3. Goldstein, A.P., *The Prepare Curriculum: Teaching Prosocial Competencies* (Champaign, Illinois: Research Press, 1988). Designed for both children and adolescents, especially those having aggressive or social withdrawal problems. The text provides detailed suggestions using games, role playing,

and group discussions to facilitate group participation and motivation. The curriculum covers areas such as problem-solving, interpersonal skills, controlling anger, managing stress, being cooperative, and dealing effectively in groups.

4. Elardo, P., & Cooper, M., *AWARE: Activities for Social Development* (Menlo Park, California: Addison-Wesley, 1977). To be used by both parents and professionals. Designed to help children understand thoughts and feelings of others, improve their ability to accept individual differences, solve interpersonal problems, and increase respect and concern for others. Can be used in small group or individual setting.

Resources for Teaching Self-Control

1. Bash, M.S., & Camp, B. *Think Aloud: Increasing Social and Cognitive Skills—A Problem-Solving Program for Children* (Champaign, Illinois: Research Press, 1985). Designed for elementary school children with guides for different grades. The goal is to achieve verbal mediation training by teaching children to verbalize plans, solutions, and consequences in cognitive and social problem situations.

2. Braswell, L., & Bloomquist, M.L., *Cognitive-Behavioral Therapy with ADHD Children* (New York: Guilford Press, 1991). Authors discuss the application of cognitive-behavioral methods with elementary children and adolescents, presenting symptoms of ADHD and/or features of oppositional defiant and conduct disorder. Detailed manual describes program for 8- to 12-year-old children.

3. Kendall, P.C., *Stop and Think Workbook* (238 Meeting House Lane, Merion Station, PA 19066, 1988). A 16-session program which provides ideas and materials to teach cognitive strategies for psychoeducational tasks, games, social problems, and how to deal effectively with emotions. Available from the author.

4. Huggins, P., *Helping Kids Handle Anger. Teaching Self-Control.* (Longmont, Colorado: Sopris West, Inc., 1990). A

very comprehensive set of lesson plans consisting of 15 lessons for both primary and intermediate students. Teaches anger is normal; there are times when it is appropriate to be angry, but we must learn to express it so that it doesn't harm others. Also emphasizes the importance of changing our "inner speech" to dampen angry responses. Tested in the classroom, but can be adapted for the counseling setting.

5. The Fourth Street Company *Stop, Relax and Think Game.* An excellent game where each player learns to verbalize feelings, practice stopping motoric action, relax and problem solve and plan ahead. Good tool for supplementing other programs. Available from (Childswork/Childsplay) Center for Applied Psychology, Inc., P.O. Box 1586, King of Prussia, PA 19406, (800) 962-1141.

6. Berg, B., *The Self-Control Game,* Cognitive-Behavioral Resources, 265 Cantebury Dr., Dayton, OH 45429. One of several games by this author. Contains pretest questionnaire that can be used to tailor content of game cards to needs of player(s). A very helpful workbook is also available to reinforce cognitive skills. Other titles include: *The Anger Control Game, and The Conduct Management Game.* Available from Childswork/Childsplay.

7. Page, P., *Getting Along.* A fun-filled set of stories, songs, and activities to help kids work and play together. (San Francisco: Children's Television Resource & Education Center, 1988). An audio tape and read-along booklet with animated stories, songs, and activities that help elementary-age children learn about issues like teasing, bullying, sharing, and respecting others.

Resources for Building Study Skills

1. DeBrueys, M.T. (Project Coordinator), *125 Ways to Be a Better Student: A Program for Study Skill Success* (Moline, Illinois: LinguiSystems 1986). A foundational text to facilitate basic study skills, and problem-solving as it relates to school survival and success in the classroom.

2. Ellis, D.B., *Becoming a Master Student* (Rapid City, South Dakota: College Survival, Inc. 1985). Written for the freshman college student, but can be adapted and translated for the junior high and high school student. Very good material on note-taking, test anxiety, and increasing memory of subject matter.

3. Scheiber, B., & Talpers, J., *Unlocking Potential: College and Other Choices for Learning Disabled People* (New York: Adler & Adler, 1987). This step-by-step guide helps adolescents decide whether or not to go to college, a technical school, or some other program. It also helps prepare them for academic hurdles and gives them strategies for adjustment, including time management and study skills.

4. *Study Smart.* A board game that is not intended to teach study skills, but rather to reinforce the use of study skills in a highly motivating way. Useful from age 10 through adolescence. Available from Childswork/Childsplay.

Videotapes
1. Copeland, E.D., *Understanding Attention Disorders* (Atlanta: 3 C's of Childhood, 1989).

2. Goldstein, S. & Goldstein, M., *Why Won't My Child Pay Attention?* A video guide for parents (Salt Lake City: Neurology, Learning and Behavior Center, 1989).

3. Goldstein, S. & Goldstein, M., *Educating Inattentive Children.* A video guide for teachers (Salt Lake City: Neurology, Learning and Behavior Center, 1990).

4. Goldstein, S. & Goldstein, M., *It's Just Attention Disorder:* A video guide for kids (Salt Lake City: Neurology, Learning and Behavior Center, 1991).

5. Phelan, T.W., *All about Attention Deficit Disorder* (Carol Stream, Illinois: Child Management, 1989).

Sources of Materials

A complete listing of books, tests, scales, and programs for ADHD children is available from *A.D.D. WareHouse,* 300 Northwest 70th Avenue, Suite 102, Plantation, FL 33317, (800) 233-9273.

Another mail order supply source for ADHD materials as well as other useful supplies for working with children is *Childswork/Childsplay,* P.O. Box 1586, King of Prussia, PA 19406, (800) 962-1141.

Organizations

1. Attention-Deficit Disorder Association (ADDA), 19262 Jamboree Blvd., Irvine, CA 92715. (800) 487-2282

2. Asthma and Allergy Foundation of America, 1717 Massachusetts Ave. NW, Suite 305, Washington, DC 20036. (202) 265-0265

3. Challenge, "A Newsletter on Attention-Deficit Hyperactivity Disorder," P.O. Box 2001, West Newbury, MA 01985. (508) 462-0495

4. Children with Attention-Deficit Disorders (CH.A.D.D.), National Headquarters, Suite 185, 1859 North Pine Island Road, Plantation, FL 33322. (305) 587-3700

5. Clearinghouse on Disability Information, U.S. Department of Education, Switzer Building, 330 C Street SW, Rm 3132, Washington, DC 20202-2524. (202) 732-1723 or 732-1241

6. Council for Exceptional Children, 1920 Association Dr., Reston, VA 22091. (703) 620-3660

7. Council for Learning Disabilities, P.O. Box 40303, Overland Park, KS 66204. (913) 492-3840

8. Christian Council on Persons with Disabilities, P.O. Box

458, Lake Geneva, WI 53147. (414) 275-6131

9. Dyslexia Research Institute, 4745 Centerville Rd., Tallahasse, FL 32308. (904) 893-2216

10. Families of Children Under Stress (FOCUS), P.O. Box 1058, Conyers, GA 30207. (404) 483-9845

11. Foundation for Attentional Disorders, 57 Pinecrest Road, Toronto, Ontario, Canada, M6P 3G6. (416) 341-1515

12. HyperActive Attention Deficit (HAAD Support Groups), P.O. Box 20563, Roanoke, VA 24018, (703) 772-0455.

13. Learning Disabilities Association of America, 4156 Library Road, Pittsburgh, PA 15234. (412) 341-1515 or 341-8077

14. National Center for Learning Disabilities, 99 Park Ave., New York, NY 10016. (212) 687-7211

15. Tourette's Syndrome Association, 42-40 Bell Blvd., Bayside, NY 11361-2861. (800) 237-0717 or (718) 224-2999